MW00439406

THE
AUTISTIC BUDDHA

My Unconventional Path to Enlightenment

THOMAS CLEMENTS

YOUR STORIES
MATTER

First published in 2017 in England by
Your Stories Matter
Revised 2018

Copyright © 2017 Thomas Clements

www.yourstoriesmatter.org
hello@yourstoriesmatter.org

Your Stories Matter is an imprint of
Explainer HQ Ltd
Halton Mill
Mill Lane
Lancaster
LA2 6ND
England

This title is available for sale online and from
loads of great bookshops worldwide.

A bulk discount is available for educational
institutions and charitable organisations
through Your Stories Matter.

British Library Cataloguing in Publication Data.
A catalogue record for this book is available
from the British Library.

Cover design by Phil Clements

ISBN 978-1-909320-58-1

All rights reserved by the publisher.

I'd like to dedicate
The Autistic Buddha to my parents,
Maria and Phil, who have shown me
infinite love and patience throughout my life,
and to my grandmother Dorothy for her
kindness in allowing me to stay with
her after returning home from Asia.
Without you, this book would not
have been possible.

"Peace comes from within.
Do not seek it without."

—*Gautama Buddha*

1. THE EARLY DAYS

AS A CHILD, when most boys of my age were out having fun together building forts in the woods or playing 'cowboys and indians' in the park, I preferred to remain on my own indoors engrossed in my beloved copies of National Geographic.

By the age of nine, I'd acquired a collection so substantial my bookshelf could no longer support the weight and subsequently collapsed on me one night while I was asleep. In my bedroom, I would while away countless hours devouring books of facts, committing hundreds of national flags and capital cities to my photographic memory. Within the confines of my room, I would often escape into an intense inner world composed of all the places I'd read about on a given day. On a Monday, maybe I'd be buying spices in the colourful bazaars of Tashkent or Samarkand. On a Thursday, perhaps I'd be trekking through dense tropical forests en route to some ancient Mayan ruins in Chihuahua. Sunday might see me pounding millet with the locals of a remote Dogon village in the depths of rural West Africa. Each night I'd spin my bedside globe and put my finger on an arbitrary spot, telling myself that when I was older I would go there.

After primary school, a period of my life I've largely erased from memory on account of being bullied pretty much the entire time, I'd fallen very much in love with all things Eastern and oriental. For me, the culture of the East had an allure like no other and offered an escape from the grim reality of being mocked, teased and beaten up in the playground every day. It was a place that was both exotic and totally unthreatening. Where things made a lot more sense to my inquisitive and adventurous young mind than in the so-called 'real world' with which, by the age of ten, I'd already become pretty disillusioned.

Growing up on the outskirts of London in a small commuter town called Epping, a place many will know as the last stop on the Central Line, I'd make regular trips on the underground to Leicester Square and then mission on to Chinatown in Soho. As I entered Gerard Street, through the big red Chinese arches, I felt as though I'd been transported to an alternate reality of *dim sum* houses, lanterns, jade Buddhas and smelly durian fruits. For a young mind besotted by travel and adventure, it offered the ultimate escape from the manicured lawns of leafy middle-class suburbia.

Chinatown was a full-on assault to my highly attuned autistic senses. Its heady atmosphere intoxicated me. Though something of a novelty to most, Chinatown was a sensory haven. Where mouth-searing chilli hot-pot bubbled away furiously next to steaming baskets of *dim sum*, and where Cantonese pop ballads and exotic-sounding dialects blared amidst the cacophony of woks and clinking porcelain crockery. As a child with a zest for travel and adventure, there was no more exciting place on Earth. It was the closest I could get to the real China, with its verdant paddies and luscious bamboo forests, a mysterious land that I had dreamt about many times over and one that seemed galaxies away from the flat and unremarkable fields of wheat and rape around Epping.

Oblivious to the world outside, for hours I'd wander aimlessly through this colourful ethnic enclave in the heart of the city: absorbing the sights and sounds, studying the contents of restaurant menus, and tasting delicious morsels of street food like *char siu bao* (sweet, fatty Chinese pork buns) and *cha ye dan* (tea-marbled eggs). I'd sit at the peace pagoda at the end of the road on my own, bubble tea in one hand bao in the other. Watching the people go by, I'd imagine myself amidst the clamour and chaos of downtown Kowloon or Mong Kok.

However, when it started to get dark—the luminous blue and red neon restaurant signs becoming brighter and the smell of soy and rice wine beginning to waft from the kitchens—a painful melancholy slipped over me. I knew it was time to head back to the suburbs and face that gloomy sense of isolation I felt as a painfully shy loner.

Unable to grasp what made the people around me tick, why none of my classmates shared the same intense interests as me and excluded me from their activities, I had developed a deep aversion to my native British culture and yearned to escape from it whenever an opportunity presented itself. I'd reluctantly hop on the tube back to middle England, where there was no street food being cooked before your eyes and where people lived uninteresting lives locked away in their leafy suburban castles. As the Tube left the city and entered suburban Essex, I recited the names of Chinese cities in my head, jotting them down in my trusty notepad which was already chock-full of long lists I'd made throughout the day. Making lists had become a thing of mine. I guess it staved off any residual anxiety by enabling my worried mind to rest and find brief respite from the capriciousness of the outside world.

Life was unorthodox for me and perhaps even a little sad. I guess the saddest thing about it was that I never really had a buddy to share my Chinatown adventures with. I never really felt privy to the world of friendship as a youngster, considering myself too eccentric, socially awkward and obsessed by stuff I knew most kids my age just wouldn't appreciate. I felt at times I would never be able to relate to anyone else in my class on quite the same wavelength. I felt like MacOS, while they were Windows 98; we operated in different ways and were very much incompatible with one another.

Fortunately, as I grew a little older, I found a few pals to knock about with at secondary school. They were all a bit odd like me. One guy was a fellow Japanophile who loved manga comics and not a lot else. The other was a hypochondriac who'd swallowed a medical dictionary and complained of a new ailment every day. I'd hang about with them at school, though I never truly enjoyed their company. At weekends I still preferred more than anything to indulge my own intense interest in the exoticism of the East. I did go to an Asian-style mall called Oriental City in Colindale with the manga fan once, but while he trawled the comic bookshop for hours, I preferred to remain in the warm embrace of the food court, breathing in the steam from bowls of ramen, imagining momentarily I was in Tokyo. We might as well have gone there separately. Even on the train journey there we didn't chat much. The only thing we did share was a packet of weird Japanese sweets on the tube home. They tasted pretty foul to be honest, kind of salty actually, and we spat them out in the bin as we changed trains at Leytonstone.

At secondary school, despite being unsuccessful in my social life, I was regularly praised by teachers for my work ethic and my unusually high level of intellectual maturity. I'd taught myself to speak fluent German by Year 11 and excelled in French and Japanese. Because of my love of cultures, I'd blossomed into quite the linguist and could absorb new vocabulary like a sponge. My ability in languages was so prodigious that by fourteen my German was indistinguishable from that of a native's.

At times however, I would obsess over my assignments, agonising over my choice of words and spend far, far too long on one to the detriment another. In terms of work, I struggled with moderation and became far too fixated about things which became a real problem for me. My grades really started to drop in Sixth Form as the workload increased.

It was the time during which I fancied myself a bit of a rebel and iconoclast in the mould of Anthony Bourdain, the rock 'n' roll author and food writer, despite being perfectly aware he was way cooler and better-looking than me. My mum, who kind of fancied him a bit, had lent me his best-selling *Kitchen Confidential*, which is still my favourite book to this day. I loved everything about it: its bawdiness, its irreverence, its vulgarity and its vivid, honest descriptions of the squalid depths of depravity he and his fellow chefs were reduced to in the restaurant kitchens of New York. More to the point, Tony had real guts and his words inspired me to step out of my comfort zone for once in my rather sheltered existence. That was, until it got me into trouble.

Arrogantly considering myself above the school system, favouring my own idiosyncratic methods of learning instead of the prescribed curriculum, I did badly in my A-Levels. OK, to tell you truth, I completely fucked them up. I even ran away from home at one point during my revision period. My distraught parents found me in a car park in Peterborough of all places.

Somehow (I'm still not sure how) I made it through the backdoor of university. Perhaps because I was clearly gifted in foreign languages. Being an autodidact hadn't always been popular with my teachers, but it had paid off. At university however, everything in my life took a dramatic turn for the worse. Years of feeling isolated from mainstream society and having little in the way of human contact had negatively impacted my emotional health. I'd barely had any proper friendships (the reclusive manga guy wasn't the sort of person who'd help you out in a crisis) or even attempted a romantic relationship (girls were strange, terrifying enigmas I did my best to avoid at school). This had evidently taken its toll on me. As a young adult, I became a psychological cripple, reaching my lowest ebb during a year abroad stint in Germany.

2. THE HOLLAND INCIDENT

I DOUBT MANY ENGLISH PEOPLE have seen the inside of a German psychiatric ward. As I lay on a hard and thoroughly uncomfortable hospital bed on the *station* (being the German word for a ward), I ruminated on whether this was some kind of achievement. Or whether it was because I was the biggest screw-up known to man. In fact I ruminated on this until the sedative the nurse had given me sent me into a heavy artificial slumber.

Life on the station wasn't as bad as one might imagine. It was a 'soft station', as my fellow mental patient Oliver informed me. Most people here were just ordinary Germans—of various ages, professions and backgrounds—who just needed time out from what can be quite a restrained and pressurized society bound by stifling conventions, typically being averse to openly expressing deep feelings and emotions. Our stays here were also voluntary and intended to be short, so straitjackets and barbarous electrical treatments weren't exactly the order of the day. Indeed, I had entered this place of my own free will after what some might describe as a 'nervous breakdown'.

At the time, I was a student a few months into my year abroad studying in Germany. For all intents and purposes I wasn't doing badly there, at least for the first part of my stay. I'd registered for my classes, attended them all and had even made a few decent acquaintances—which was certainly not easy for someone like me—mainly expats and foreign exchange students. They were a generally chummy, multicultural bunch of people with whom I shared fleeting yet fond experiences: like a trip to the local Becks factory, a day of coffee tasting at one of the city's oldest cafes, and an excursion to some cranky Iron Age reenactment village outside the city (I considered myself nerdy, but the dudes that ran that place were on another level entirely).

Something was amiss however, and I could feel it building inside of me as each day passed. It almost felt physical, like a demon insidiously working its way into the fabric of my being, tearing its way through my inner peace and tranquillity. In reality, it was a build-up of tension that had been going on for years. Now, in Germany, it was bubbling to the surface and coming to a head, when for once in my life I was actually feeling relatively sane and functional.

For some inexplicable reason, I decided to withdraw from everything. I squandered every good thing that I'd built in my new home of Germany, and retreated into a cocoon of duvets and a world of fantasy limited to the confines of my bedroom. Instead of getting up in the mornings and taking the tram to campus, I stayed in bed. Instead of cooking or eating meals of bratwurst and sauerkraut at the student canteen, I hoarded pretzels, paprika chips and bottles of apple juice in my room. Instead of attending lectures, I watched back-to-back documentaries on YouTube on topics ranging from Kintsugi, the ancient Japanese art of repairing pottery, to introductions to Taoism by the philosopher Alan Watts—deliberately picking things that had absolutely nothing to do with my immediate surroundings nor had any relevance to my degree. Instead of going out with friends, I jealously viewed the pictures on Facebook of their shopping trips to Hamburg and their fun-filled antics at the annual carnival in Wiesbaden. I'm not really sure what happened, but it's as though a fuse blew in my head. My body became listless and exhausted, and I could no longer cope with even the most prosaic of tasks.

Things got really bad eight weeks into my self-imposed isolation when, after a sleepless night, I broke free from my miserable stasis and my squalid little bedroom which had become a landfill site of empty Becks bottles (some filled with pee from when I couldn't even be bothered to go to the toilet), half-eaten stale, mouldy sausages and piles of unwashed clothes. Foolishly, I boarded a train early in the morning for the Dutch city of Groningen—Bremen wasn't far from the German border with Holland, which meant one thing in my tiny little mind: weed. Yes, I had planned it all in my highly confused, blinkered and irresponsibly naïve state. I'd hop on the express train to Holland, find a coffee shop, bring back a big bag of weed and all my problems would magically disappear. How wrong I was to prove to be.

You see, despite being twenty two at the time, I'd never tried this supposedly mind-expanding drug that many of my fellow students lauded as just about the best thing since chocolate ice cream for its ability to send its users into a blissful state of calm and spiritual transcendence. I guess that, being an awkward type with really dreadful social skills, I'd never been able to access the typical venues, like parties or raves, where the drug was being offered around. So, in my typically inept and socially naïve style, I decided to enter *De Glory*, a coffee shop in the centre of a charming, inoffensive Dutch city of canals, cheese shops, potted tulips and half-timbered merchant houses. The place was awful, a real den of iniquity, blasting out death metal and billowing cannabis smoke at ten in the morning. Its presence was totally incongruous in amongst the city's picturesque and quaint surroundings. I felt ashamed to even be in there and even more so when I approached the bartender—a greasy-haired, stinky, drug-addled biker in his forties—and asked him for a joint. When he gave me what I had long-harboured an intense curiosity to try, I felt like I was getting away with something and it gave me a rush.

Unfortunately, that rush combined with several nights' sleep deprivation, toking my joint far too quickly, and what I had reluctantly acknowledged to be a deep depression, all culminated in a terrifying panic attack. I felt my heartbeat race like never before. I felt the ground move underneath me. I felt like my head was being filled with some gassy incendiary fluid and was going to explode. I felt like something imminent and disastrous was about to happen. It was indescribably horrific.

I stumbled outside of *De Glory*, hoping that a brisk walk and some bracing February air would alleviate the awful feelings. Instead, it only served to make them worse and my heartbeat seemed to get faster as a feeling of death began to loom over me. I was somehow convinced, in my state of panic and confusion, that I was facing the unknown and must quickly atone for my militant atheism and past sins. It was truly terrifying at the time, and yet utterly ridiculous when I look back on it. Passers-by must have thought I was a lunatic: a bumbling, weed-addled English interloper amidst a calm and composed Dutch public going about its daily business of buying gouda and *stoopwafels*, stumbling all over the cobbled pavement, hyperventilating and carrying on like I was close to death. I remember getting to a park, and a brief spell of writhing in agony on a bench I'd collapsed onto with my eyes fully closed, hoping this terrifying episode would end.

Eventually I arrived, after several kilometres traipsing in the bitter cold snow, at a bus station where I summoned the courage to ask a girl for help. I'm not sure what help I expected to receive, but I felt as though I needed somebody to at least reassure me everything was going to be okay. Initially the girl's look spoke of bewilderment and she responded incredulously to my plea: *Is this some kind of joke? Are you for real?* I think at first she thought about pushing me away. However, while somehow aware I wasn't a medical emergency, she soon realised something was up—perhaps that I wasn't quite right upstairs—and calmly guided me to the warm embrace of a sandwich shop inside the station waiting area. A Dutch boy with striking blonde curly hair who spoke the most perfectly enunciated English I've ever heard asked me what was up, to which I responded like a gibbering idiot: *I smoked some cannabis and now I'm dying. I think I've had some sort of allergic reaction.* Without hesitation, he shouted to his colleague *WATER!* (pronounced *vah-tuhr* in Dutch) and proceeded to put his arm around me.

After the panic I'd experienced and the cold indifference of passers-by, I really regarded this young man— who was most likely just an average student with a stultifying part-time job at a crappy little sandwich shop in a bus station—as an angel sent from heaven. He reassured me all would be well and I truly believed him. After what seemed like a brief respite, as I sat down at one of the tables and sipped water from a disposable plastic cup, an ambulance arrived. Two big burly guys, they must have been about six foot five, in fluorescent orange approached me and, in good English with a distinctive Dutch lilt, told me they just needed to check me out.

After a quick check of my vitals, I appeared to be fine. By that time I'd sort of calmed down and was even able to chuckle with the ambulance men as they assuaged my completely irrational fears that I wasn't dying. I even apologised to them for not being able to speak Dutch, for smoking weed and for rudely ignoring the wealth of Holland's cultural options I could have chosen instead. Po-faced, they told me to eat something sweet, preferably some nice Dutch chocolate from the artisanal chocolatier down the road, and then go home. They slammed the ambulance door behind me as I faced the derision of the entire bus station who'd watched me make a fool of myself.

As I approached the shop owner, a moustachioed Middle Easterner with an inane toothy grin, and asked him for a Snickers bar, he replied: *Do you want hashish with that?* Humiliated, I dragged my sorry arse back to Bremen. The train back was a slow one. The residual feelings of panic and strange, tingling, electric-like sensations began to subside. I arrived back home in Bremen after one of the most surreal and unexpected events perhaps ever. I flopped on the bed and an overwhelming exhaustion kicked in.

After twenty hours or so of being knocked out, I woke up in a daze with a pounding headache. I couldn't remember a damn thing from the previous day, until I scratched my chest and peeled off a sticky electrode. What the hell? Oh, fuck, yes, I remember now: the ECG, the ambulance, the bus station, the wandering around a foreign city in the bitter cold telling myself I was going to die. Fuck! It all came flooding back. I felt highly embarrassed and thoroughly ashamed of myself for what I'd put myself through.

Trying to restore some semblance of normality, after what I had rationalised to be a blip and something of an embarrassing scrape, I vowed with grim determination to tidy my room, attend classes after a long inexcusable absence and stop ignoring calls from mates. First thing first though: shower. I stank, having slept in my clothes after smoking cannabis and wandering aimlessly in a state of terror around a Dutch city for several hours.

However, my brief resolve was soon obliterated by the intrusion of what I realised to be another panic attack. Fuck, fuck, FUCK! I did my best to control it, but it became so intense I wanted to burst into tears. The feeling that one's heart is about to explode and one's very existence is being threatened by an evil force is indescribably horrific. A warm soapy shower did nothing to placate or comfort me.

My landlord at the time, Uwe (pronounced *Oo-vah*), a whip-thin middle-aged man in unfashionable round retro glasses, was staying at the *Wohngemeinschaft* (basically a big house shared by eight or so students). He noticed something wasn't right about me. As I sat tapping on my desk desperately wishing for the panic to disappear, Uwe, who always wore sandals indoors, hovered outside my room. He instinctively knew something was up and peered into my room. Realising I looked in a bad way, in a characteristically straightforward and unsentimental German way, he asked me: *Was ist los mit dir?* (What the hell's up with you?) I told him everything. Upon realising I was clearly going through agony, he immediately softened his brusque German demeanour and guided me calmly downstairs, outside and into his burgundy VW Polo.

After a short wait in the face-searingly cold reception area of the central hospital (the heating had broken down on one of the coldest nights of the year), I managed to see a doctor. A really stern and intimidating one. For whatever reason, I burst into a flood of tears and dissolved into a snotty mess in front of the immaculately groomed physician before me. He was an old-fashioned type in a reassuring white coat who exuded an exceptionally cold, creepy, intellectual aura. He diagnosed depression almost straight away, without so much as eye contact. He recommended Uwe drive me to a hospital, one that specialised in psychiatric disorders at the other end of the city, a fair way from where I was living.

After an hour's wait, this time in a nice warm seating area with piped elevator music, an unusually gentle, kind-hearted female psychiatrist called Lena sat me down and asked me what was wrong. I told her everything, to the best of my ability, in German: including the two months spent isolated in my room and the Holland incident. Before long, I was to become acquainted with another 'station' with the help of a very kind, softly spoken nurse. This place was to be my new home for eight confusing, painful, heart-breaking and occasionally life-affirming weeks.

3. THE MENTAL PATIENT

LIFE ON THE STATION began quite predictably and played out a bit like a scene from *One Flew Over the Cuckoo's Nest*, except as inpatients we were allowed to wear our civilian outfits as opposed to some ugly institution gown. After a drab breakfast of rye bread and quark (a kind of spreadable farmers cheese with what to me was an unpalatably sour taste), we had a *Morgenrunde*. Here patients would sit round in a circle and moan about all things: ranging from how empty they felt and how futile existence was, to the explosive yellow-coloured diarrhoea they were having from their new medication (bear in mind we'd just eaten breakfast). As I sat there, I began imagining myself as Jack Nicholson's character in the film, albeit in some bizarre alternate German reality where discussing bowel movements in gruesome detail straight after having eaten was a perfectly normal and acceptable thing to do.

A few of the patients around me looked visibly sicker than me. Many were pallid from a lack of decent nutrition (well, what nourishment is there in quark?), frail from inactivity, dark-ringed around the eyes from countless disturbed nights' sleep, and with misery and neurosis etched in their faces. It was truly a sad sight indeed to see people reduced to this state. Life has a habit of being harsher on some more than others, I thought. Some in the morning round just seemed a bit down, but still had sufficient energy to muster a faint smile and a light chuckle. But who was I to judge what was going on inside their heads? I wasn't privy to their thoughts or the inner-workings of their psyche after all.

As for me, I felt calmer. The high dose of lorazepam they gave me prior to entering the ward definitely helped. In fact, I felt more relaxed than I had ever before—almost immune from harm. But of course sedatives have a habit of wearing off very quickly and, soon after leaving the *Morgenrunde*, I felt the ground beneath me moving. Shit. What was happening? An earthquake perhaps? No, just another panic attack. Another fucking panic attack. This was becoming something of a routine. As adrenaline rushed through my body, time seemed to freeze and people around me appeared to move in slow motion. It was surreal, like being in a dream—a really bad one. This, I came to learn, is what they call *derealisation*, a common symptom associated with anxiety. From the all-out fear I was experiencing, I quickly descended into what I can only describe as a vortex of despair and an indescribably painful feeling of emptiness. I burst into an uncontrollable fit of crying.

Fellow patients, notably two dishevelled skinny men I'd already dismissed as lost causes and loonies, stared in disbelief as two nurses (one a butch Turkish man with fat hairy arms) calmed me and held my shaking hands, while another (a benign-looking female nurse, also Turkish) brought me a cup of water and another sedative pill. This one was bright orange and looked a lot stronger than the first one they'd given me. It was. I calmed right down. The two male patients who'd gawked at me just shrugged their shoulders and walked off. Other patients treated me with cold indifference, as though my episode was not even worthy of their acknowledgment. Except for Oliver, my soon-to-be good pal, who wore an empathetic pained expression on witnessing my suffering.

Oliver was an ex-reporter for a national German newspaper (he wasn't just saying this either, he showed me many of the articles he'd written and his official ID). The cut-throat world of journalism hadn't treated him well however. In his reporter ID photo he looked a robustly handsome man with chiselled features, slicked back hair and beautiful wrinkle-free skin. Now in person, after a series of personal tragedies and the onset of a massive breakdown, he looked frazzled, burnt-out and ravaged by inner-turmoil and suffering. He told me he was thirty nine, but he looked much older. His teeth were brown and rotting, his skin dry and pitted. He presented perhaps the worst example of what depression can do to a person, yet he still managed to exude a warmth and compassion able to touch me beyond words.

He was sympathetic to my panic attack and did his best to distract me from it by asking me questions, while brewing me a nice cup of camomile tea. He chose to address me in English (I'd been speaking in German to everyone the rest of the time), after I'd introduced myself as a Brit during the *Morgenrunde*. Turned out he was quite the anglophile, and a highly cultured and educated one at that. His knowledge of English monarchs, the geology of the Lake District and the streets of London put me to shame. We quickly became good pals on the ward and, while time here passed for what seemed like an eternity, our conversations about the world, its people, its food and its problems kept us both going.

Oliver was an old school depressive. Not a thin-skinned panicky wreck like me, but a world-weary, cynical and disillusioned type who, it turned out, had abused drugs and alcohol throughout his chequered career. As a reporter, he had been sent to the back of beyond, to war zones and to places most will probably never even have heard of. He'd tried nearly every type of drug, from Guatemalan hallucinogens to Somalian *khat*. When I opened up about my rather lightweight encounter with cannabis in Holland—the event which brought me to hospital—he could barely keep a straight face. I couldn't blame him. It was pretty funny looking back on it, but the state it had left me in certainly wasn't.

I was ill. Really ill. Panic attacks and depression had consumed every cell in my body. Naturally when one is ill one agrees, or is often coaxed, to try medication. This is what I did. The ward's psychiatrist, a portly rosy-cheeked psychiatrist who spoke in a gravelly harsh Bavarian accent, put me on citalopram (pretty much the standard antidepressant for those starting out on the pill route). He assured me in his thickly accented German that this would address both the panic and the crippling lows of depression I'd been experiencing in my isolation. Depression and panic disorder were now my diagnoses: two conditions not uncommon in people with autistic traits, who by nature are often highly-strung and emotionally sensitive. I was certainly emotionally sensitive. I'm not much into psychoanalysing myself, but I guess it went back to being bullied at school. But what difference did any of that make now? I just had to do whatever I could to get well again and no amount of ruminating on the past was going to change that.

Back on the ward I asked the nursing staff (who, much like in the films, sat behind the Perspex window of a nursing station surreptitiously observing the patients and then logging their behaviour) what I should be doing to aid my recovery. They all told me to distract myself by playing a board or card game (Rummy seemed to be a favourite on the ward), and to simply wait for the medication to kick in. For a while, I really did believe that this pill would cure me and that I would soon—perhaps in a matter of days or weeks—be able to put this little blip behind me and function normally again, attend classes and start enjoying life with my expat friends. That wasn't to be the case. In fact, it was to be quite the opposite.

4. THE STATION

TEN DAYS HAD PASSED on the station. Breakfasts alternated between rye with sweaty sausage, stinky Emmenthal, and the ubiquitous quark (something I was oddly beginning to acquire a taste for). The *Morgenrunde* remained pretty much the same. We all bitched about how miserable we felt, how exhausted we were, and how runny or discoloured our poo was. The nurses in attendance would furiously take notes, yet offer little in the way of solutions to our existential angst and inner turmoil other than playing Rummy, Monopoly or Checkers. If that wasn't helping, at most they'd suggest to the portly Bavarian in charge that we change our medication. A change of medication was about the most exciting thing a psychiatric inpatient could look forward to. It offered more hope than any of the conventional, talking group-based therapies, or the less conventional qigong and yoga exercises the hospital also offered as a side.

The lady leading these extra sessions was a tetchy, and at times thoroughly irritating, self-styled, New Age, spiritual self-help guru. Even the lowliest of the depressives in our motley group were incredulous to the idea that our chakras needed realigning and our qi rebalancing. If anything, the sessions (which began with a five minute meditation set to some drossy panpipe music) provided light relief. On the yoga mat, for instance, we were encouraged to adopt a lotus position. In truth, most of us were so woefully unfit that we lacked the dexterity to even maintain a semi-lotus. One time, upon observing our struggle, I got the giggles, mainly fuelled by the fact the instructor took it all dead seriously. Now the group, which like most Germans was normally a staid bunch, became infected by my chuckling and the room quickly descended into childlike anarchy. It completely undermined our snappy pashmina-wearing instructor who, despite preaching the importance of calm and tranquillity, seethed with a palpable rage. It pissed her off big time. In that brief moment all our fears, petty apprehensions and depressive thoughts were lifted; and I think all of us felt a temporary relief from being ourselves.

That was until we had to face the grim drudgery of ward life again. Medication now seemed like a good option, an easy one that didn't involve anything as tedious as looking inwards and extirpating any demons which had rooted themselves in our fragile minds. A simple pill promised a way to mask the pain we were all feeling and a way to alter those pesky chemical imbalances in our brains which were supposedly causing us to feel bad. I stayed on citalopram for a while. Drug connoisseur Oliver on the other hand had run the gamut of antidepressants and yet felt no discernible effect from any of them. He was of the rather simplistic and conspiratorial view that psych-meds, and the giant pharmaceutical concerns that made them, were merely out to extort the vulnerable and those who knew no better. He maintained these drugs were designed to numb rather than heal. I guess there was a kernel of truth in what he believed. But I still clung on to the hope that one of the medications may just lift me out of the panic and despair that now enveloped me like *a black tortilla of depression around a pain burrito*—to quote Christopher Moore, the American fantasy writer.

It had got to the stage I now avoided even going to the Ghanaian-owned internet café around the corner from the hospital (the two black guys who owned it spoke English to me and were far more chilled than the Germans) for fear of the ground beneath me shaking and for fear of being sucked into another despair-vortex (they were the nearest thing to hell on earth, save perhaps for Harlow or Basildon). Medication seemed like a way better option than qigong and yoga anyhow (for one thing, it had the potential to do something other than just make me laugh).

After a little over two weeks, the citalopram really started to kick in. I felt a little better, but not nearly as good as I'd hoped. It dulled the pain of depression, though I could still feel it lurking just beneath the surface, ready and waiting to strike when I was feeling at my most vulnerable. Citalopram also helped soften the frequent blows dealt to my frazzled nerves by panic attacks, which had since reduced to maybe once every other day. It didn't, however, eliminate them or their root cause completely.

Unfortunately, the side effects were a bit brutal and, now suffering them myself, I felt a little more sympathy for the relentless whining of my fellow patients at the *Morgenrunde*. I too felt like whining and did so much more often now. Despite eating less, mainly due to the stodgy uninspiring slops they served us at the hospital, I inexplicably started to pile on the pounds. The German equivalent of Nurse Ratched, who was perhaps even more dour and odious than the film character, told me that I didn't exercise enough. She was notorious for giving glib and patronising advice that made you feel wholly inadequate. Another nurse (a much nicer, gentler tubby chap), in whom everyone would confide if they had a problem, told me these drugs affect the metabolism and can cause unexpected weight gain. Quite a few of my fellow inpatients I'd noticed had an unhealthy, bloated look about them and I was slowly becoming one of them. I didn't like it one bit. My stool, though thankfully not that hideous yellowy colour they'd been describing, was dark and runny. Having lost any of my inhibitions and pride (which to me now seemed vastly overrated and point-less), I described this to the group. Most remained un-perturbed with a glazed look, apart from one other guy who, like me, had started on citalopram and who, like me, was suffering from really bad diarrhoea.

It was to prove just about the only thing we had in common. He was a former waiter from the Rhineland who, for whatever reason, took a real dislike to me and made a conscious effort to avoid any possible conversa-tion with me on the ward. I tried not to take offence and thought that maybe he had had a few bad experiences in his native Boppard with a coachload of coarse tattooed Brits—from places like Stockport or Cleethorpes—who'd arrived at his restaurant without a reservation in the mid-dle of a busy lunch service, ordered their food in English and then proceeded to hum the Dambusters theme tune. With that in mind, I couldn't blame him for hating me. Or perhaps he just hated the way I looked. Or perhaps he recognised I was a bit different—a bit socially awkward.

Having felt less bound by social constraints than back home in England, by playing a strangely liberating role as a bungling foreigner here in Germany, I thrived socially; even despite this terrible episode I was going through. My marked eccentricity, woeful grasp of nu-ance, verbal cues and body language, and my infamously brutal honesty all proved to be irrelevant in Germany. In fact the honesty part proved to be, if anything, a strength here. Germans aren't especially big on nuance either, and their language contains little of the mind-bending double-meanings and confusing idioms for which English is famed. In that sense, the German language is more suitable for a mind like mine, even though it perhaps lacks the spontaneity and colour I adore in poetry by the likes of Keats and Wordsworth.

Germany is also arguably a more egalitarian society than the UK, so being an eccentric doesn't make you feel a lesser individual or a freak. Germans have more or less moved beyond that petty-mindedness. Because of this, I started to open up and thrive on the ward for a while, where a cross section of German society were a captive audience for honing my newly discovered social skills. Instead of feeling ostracised and rejected, I felt warmly received by Germans who looked beyond my idiosyncrasies and actually appreciated my passion for their language and culture. Forcing me in close proximity to others for the entire day, the ward prevented me from retreating into destructive self-absorption by making routine isolation and withdrawal from the world impossible. Though I spent the majority of my time speaking to Oliver, my intellectual and cultural peer, I had gained a reputation as quite the chatterbox. This had to have been a first in my largely singular twenty four years of existence. Loquacity never came easy to me in England, but it did in Germany. For an all-too-brief time, I felt pretty good. Well, even. I started to feel I could eventually find a way out of the rabbit hole I'd fallen down. That was until I had a terrifying thought. This time however, I wasn't having a panic attack.

After three weeks on Station 61, I realised I had to face the daunting prospect of letting my university know what had happened. They had to know the truth about everything. The whole staying in bed for two months, missing half a semester's worth of lectures, the unfortunate incident in Holland, the panic attacks, the citalopram, the fact that I'd voluntarily checked myself into a psychiatric hospital. Dropping a bombshell as big as this on them certainly wasn't going to be easy.

But contrary to what I'd thought, the university took everything rather well. They waived my year abroad requirements and told me not to worry about my workload and instead to concentrate on getting better. This was an enormous relief. I could stay here for a while, courtesy of my medical insurance, get better, practise my German while I was doing so and, most importantly for me at the time, stay near to my friend Oliver. The night I'd received the news from Nottingham, he and I celebrated by leaving the ward for a few hours spontaneously. We were allowed to do that here, so long as we were back by lights out at 11pm.

Elated, we hopped on to one of Bremen's eastbound trams to the trendy gentrified area known simply as *Das*

Viertel (The District). It was kind of like Shoreditch, but less pretentious with fewer hipsters and less ironic facial hair. People here were trendier and better-looking than average, without being totally wrapped up in their own ludicrous self-image. I'd read somewhere about a place here that I knew I would like, and was sure Oliver would appreciate too: a Vietnamese restaurant (we'd spent hours talking about *Apocalypse Now*, one of our favourite films, so it made sense). It turned out that Oliver himself, though German through and through and overtly proud of it, had a Vietnamese grandmother. And upon close inspection of his beautiful face, you could definitely see an Asiatic look around his big, slightly almond-shaped eyes. I'm certain he could attribute his good looks to that drop of eastern blood in his Germanic gene pool. He really had a sculpted face. He did admit though, despite being a globetrotter in his past life, he knew practically nothing of his ancestral culture. I therefore relished the opportunity, as the previously lone Chinatown explorer of my youth, to finally share an experience of East Asia with someone other than myself by reacquainting Oliver with the cuisine of his forefathers. The reality was something far less romantic and sentimental however.

I couldn't put my finger on what it was, but for some strange reason, after extricating ourselves from the oppressive clutches of the station, we didn't feel the rush of excitement we'd expected. On the tram, attempting to merge with a highly ordered, streamlined and efficient German public, we both looked dishevelled and a bit pathetic, like two lowly street urchins in Victorian Mayfair. Our grandiose chats on the ward and air of intellectual superiority faded into irrelevance as we merged with the waves of rush hour commuters en route to Das Viertel. We both became self-conscious and a bit sheepish, as though everyone around us knew that we'd both come out of the looney bin for a brief excursion. It felt a bit like my old days of being painfully shy and awkward, struggling to find a topic of conversation or make a connection with those around me.

Upon arriving at our destination, I tried to remedy this conspicuously tense feeling between us by lauding the cuisine of Vietnam and doing my best to convey the aromatic spices using every adjective I could remember from my schoolboy German vocab book. It did nothing. Oliver's cold inertia made me uneasy. I really don't know why it was like this, especially given we'd gotten on so well before. Maybe it was just a bad omen for what was to come. The restaurant, which promised to be so authentic as to make you feel you'd eaten a hot steaming bowl of pho on a floating market by the Mekong, was actually just some pretentious faux-Asian mockery of a place. The fare was gloopy and *gringofied*, as chef Bourdain would say, with dishes like electric pink sweet and sour pork laden with corn flour, and greasy spring rolls that had come straight from a packet. Even the pho, the iconic Vietnamese soup noodle dish, was merely a bowl of instant ramen, a few manky coriander leaves, and chicken so dry we both almost choked to death on the stringy white protein strands. To top it off, the chefs were Germans. Ex-backpackers who'd been to Vietnam, tasted the food and thought they could replicate it at home without bothering to learn how to first chop vegetables or use a wok.

The whole thing was a friggin' disaster and couldn't have played out any worse. We barely talked to each other and the awful food compounded our depression. What little we did say to one and other was stilted and formal. Mainly things about the Vietnam War, which descended into a lot of tedious Noam Chomsky-inspired tirades on American war crimes and imperialism. I'd had enough. We'd both had enough. In fact, Oliver even admitted he'd rather have just eaten a doner kebab round the corner from the hospital.

I felt disheartened by it all. What seemed like a ripe opportunity to finally share with somebody my obsession for all things eastern disintegrated into an evening both of us would rather forget. I didn't give up on it despite the bad air between us, but my vain attempts at superficial chit-chat were futile and only fuelled this feeling of gross inadequacy and ineptitude at making reasonable conversation. I felt as though I'd merely burdened Oliver with my company because, after all, I'd invited him and failed to be a convivial host.

We arrived back at the ward sodden. Almost by fate, it had started to rain buckets after leaving the restaurant. Upon arrival, we exchanged a terse *Gute Nacht* and returned to our respective rooms. I felt shitty about it all. To top it all, Oliver went out drinking the following night with a fellow patient. He didn't even ask me to come. I felt heartbroken, as though that indescribably wonderful and life-affirming connection one feels in friendship had been snatched away from me in an instant, without adequate explanation.

After a soothing hot shower, I lay in bed reading, as I often did: Shakespeare's *As You Like It*. I'd never been into literature, unless it was non-fiction, but vowed to improve my knowledge of my country's own literary behemoth by reading his entire oeuvre during my hospital stay. Hell, I had a lot of time on my hands. I guess it was a covert form of patriotism. The famous *all the world's a stage* quote stuck in my mind as I shut the book and switched off my reading lamp. The world was indeed a stage and I, like everyone, was playing a part. But mine was surely of the eternal loser, not the part I thought I'd auditioned for.

After that night I became withdrawn, averse to much contact with others. Resentfulness kicked in, jealousy even, as I watched others chat, laugh and connect with one another on a human level that I found difficult to access. With this negativity the panic attacks, quite unsurprisingly, worsened. Despite now being able to recognise the symptoms before they became full-blown episodes, the sense of sheer terror they elicited remained the same.

One morning, during our short group walk (or *Spaziergang*) around the hospital gardens, panic hit me round the face like a slap, without prior warning or any identifiable sign of a trigger. The cold mid-February air froze our fingers and our extremities. It was so unpleasant that none of us wanted to be outside. The birds in the aviary had even stopped singing and the whiteness of the snow that carpeted the ground was blinding. The atmosphere was eerie and the grey sky overhead was pressure-heavy and oppressive. Something, maybe the atmosphere and the cold, brought on the mother of all panic attacks. While the group remained oblivious, I grabbed hold of a nearby tree for dear life. Then, before long, the despair-vortex sucked me in once again, this time with a lot more force. And then came the incessant, uncontrollable undignified fits of crying and hand-flapping. All of this happened in plain view of the other patients, a bearded ex-hippie social worker who accompanied us, and the poor freezing birds in the aviary.

There really was neither rhyme nor reason to these fits of acute, unbridled anxiety and depression. During my weekly visit with the portly psychiatrist (someone without a single ounce of human warmth or emotion), I mentioned I'd had another attack and that I wanted them to stop. He would of course put the ball back in my court by asking me in an incredulous voice what I thought triggered them. I would respond there was no trigger, they just happened. We continued to remain at odds on this matter.

As the weeks passed, I noticed very little improvement in my overall well-being. The doctor's natural recourse was to up the dosage of citalopram by 20mg each time. Goodie. More drugs along with more weight gain and perhaps even the promise of that yellow diarrhoea the others complained of. While I did agree to up my intake, like Oliver I grew disillusioned about the efficacy of anti-depressants and psychiatry in general. Psychiatrists were good on jargon, diagnoses, symptoms and analysing behaviours, but seemed pretty useless when it came to offering actual solutions. It all seemed unscientific, unmethodical and more like random guesswork as far as I could tell.

However, this increased sense of disillusionment did at least get me closer to Oliver again. As for that fateful evening in Das Vierte, turns out it wasn't all my fault after all. Oliver had been having a bad day himself and the change of scene was a bit much for him. It didn't excuse the bad food, but it made me feel ten times better. Maybe I wasn't as socially inept as I thought.

Our disillusionment with the ward often just dissolved into platitudinous, freshman-grade conversations
about existence, the horrors of global capitalism and
some brief flirtations with some embarrassingly dumb-
ass conspiracy theories (Oliver was himself a recovering
conspiracy theorist, which perhaps partly explained why
his career at the national newspaper had gone awry).
Anyway, bitching about things—however petty or prim-
itive—was about the best therapy on offer in what I'd
come to see was a many-roomed building masquerading
as a hospital with psychiatrists in white coats masquerading as doctors.

Oliver and I code-switched between English and German. It was our way of confusing the non-English speaking nursing staff and it amused us both. Our friendship
certainly wasn't approved of by the ghoulish Nurse
Ratched imitator, who'd frequently interrupt and derail
our conversations by mentioning something prosaic like
what time dinner was or that one of us hadn't made our
bed. It was her vain attempt to bring us back down to
earth, but it didn't work as we'd just laugh it off. Using
both languages made us feel dynamic, in a ward that was
in dire need of some creative spark.

One of the best things about Oliver was that he wasn't
easily offended. This was lucky, because God had missed
including something vital between my mind and my
mouth. My brutally honest style seemed to appeal to

him. It was probably an antidote to years of grinning and bearing the smarmy insincerity of fellow journalists. The main thing though was that we were pals and we worked well together.

He allowed me to unload vast amounts of information on arcane topics in which I had an intense level of interest (something I hadn't learned to tone down by that age). And, in appreciation for not shunning me for being a boring little tit, I indulged his proclivity to turn otherwise sensible topics into some infuriatingly simplistic theory about the operations of a shadowy, clandestine elite pulling all the strings of all the world's major institutions (including the newspaper he'd worked for) from behind the scenes.

We were both oddballs, and we found each others' foibles endearing rather than annoying. So the day Oliver was told out of the blue—by the bespectacled, bearded sandal-wearing ex-hippie—that they'd found him a flat and could now receive floating support outside the hospital, I was gutted. In my heart of hearts, I knew I wasn't well enough to leave the hospital myself. The panic attacks were bad, the depression at times even worse than before, and the feeling of exhaustion was almost unbearable. And now, without Oliver there on the ward, it all seemed a bit pointless. The morning he left, he'd shaved for the first time I'd known him. He looked about ten years younger.

We exchanged the briefest of goodbyes and he gestured to hug me. This is something I'd dreaded. I struggle with physical contact, especially overt displays of affection, but I did it anyway, putting my arms and head awkwardly in the wrong places as I did so. It didn't matter though because we were friends and Oliver knew I was, well, a bit different to the average individual. When he exited the ward, with his lime green military-style haversack hanging over his left shoulder, I suppressed a flood of tears and proceeded to lock myself in the small bathroom outside. This was a dirty little smokers' loo, sullied by ash and covered in cigarette butts, where presumably there wasn't a smoke alarm. I collapsed on my knees onto the filthy floor, curled up in a foetal ball and wept. Would I see him again? Was that the end of my one true friendship? Was what we had even considered a friendship in the eyes of most people? In any case, I didn't feel like I wanted to carry on any more.

5. BACK TO SQUARE ONE

TIREDNESS, chronic exhaustion in fact, had become my chief symptom. I wasn't just listless, I felt overwhelmed by even the smallest exertion. Without Oliver there to distract me, I increasingly focussed on how bad I felt, inevitably making it worse. Being on a psychiatric ward for an extended period of time encourages, and eventually forces, you to dwell on your illness in an unhealthy way, that isn't remotely conducive to recovery. Patients who had been on Station 61 for a long time, some as long as eighteen months, had fallen into the futile pattern of dwelling on how bad their headaches were and noticing alarming twinges in their chest and arms that previously hadn't existed.

It was inevitable I guess that after six weeks of largely bumming about, drinking excessive amounts of camomile tea (I was told it was a natural anxiety reliever and nerve tonic by Nurse Ratched the 2nd), occasionally venturing downstairs when my anxiety permitted to buy a cappuccino-flavoured Ritter Sport bar (the highlight of my day once Oliver had left), I had become, or was at least starting to become, one of them—the institutionalised lot. I had vowed at the start that I would make an exit plan. But complacency had led me to feel content as one of the animals, living as a lab rat constantly being peered at, scrutinised by and written about by technicians hiding in a locked room behind a window. I'd grown used to set feeding, walking and medication times. The latter was the highlight of a lot of people's day, as they'd queue up at the hatch and receive their cup of pill and cup of water. It was soul-destroying to watch, never mind being part of, day in, day out.

Life was abnormal here, and this abnormality seemed blatantly apparent now I was facing it head on without Oliver there for light relief. Realising that patients weren't so much recovering as being drugged and placated indefinitely, I swallowed the bitter pill of truth that such illnesses, especially depressive ones, weren't really that treatable and all places such as these offered was nothing more than continual false hope. True, I hadn't tinkered with my medication or given the prescribed therapies much of a chance, but I knew from what I observed in the other patients that I'd probably be wasting my life and rotting my brain even more if I did.

Unsurprisingly, my decision to check out of Station 61 wasn't met with great resistance by our psychiatrist. In fact, he seemed relieved at the prospect of me leaving. I'd asked too many questions and hadn't cooperated nearly enough. I left the ward after eight weeks, not feeling resentful in the slightest. If anything I felt like a richer person for the experience. But I knew I still wasn't well. The exhaustion was worse now, to the point even the walk from the hospital door to the bus stop seemed daunting. My depression had morphed into something much more physically debilitating, but I knew a hospital was not the place for me to fight this. Despite my resolve to find a solution, I felt too tired to do anything, even to go and find Oliver at his new flat. This was bad. Really bad.

6. OVER MY HEAD AND UNDER THE RADAR

MY ROOM on *Bodelschwingstrasse* was in exactly the same state of squalor I had left it eight weeks ago on that bitingly cold night. It felt surreal to be back. Dust had accumulated on the blinds and bookshelves. Mouldy food remains had turned into grey powders, previously wet laundry had hardened, and half-drunk bottles of Mezzo Mix (a German soft drink like cola but with a citrus twist) had gone flat.

I sat down on my stained uncovered mattress and took stock of the series of bizarre and unfortunate events that had taken place. It all seemed maddeningly incomprehensible. I decided to simply lie down with my eyes closed and listen to the ceaseless drone of traffic outside. I put on one of my eye masks to block the light that filtered through my dusty metallic blinds and focussed on the incessant whir of the passing cars. The monotony was broken by mellifluous birdsong which, if I'd listened to it long enough, might have induced me into a near transcendental state of serenity. It was remarkable that even in such shitty circumstances I had managed to find an oasis of sorts, a temporary one at least, that helped me drift into a gentle, semi-conscious reverie. This wasn't to last however. I was soon to be rudely awoken by a loud, brain-jarring pounding on my bedroom door.

It was Uwe, the landlord, and he was demanding payment for the rent. The same guy who had been kind enough to take pity on me all those nights ago, during my appallingly vulnerable, panic-stricken state, had now turned into a miserly Shylock creature devoid of human sensibility. Well, almost. To be fair, I did owe him a lot of money and he had every right to be pissed off. Mental illness and a stay in the looney bin didn't absolve me of basic responsibilities like paying for a place to stay. Upon payment of my rent, I tidied, swept and dusted my sordid little man cave and went out to get a haircut, a shave and to reclaim a little self-respect.

With frizzy untamed hair and an unflatteringly fluffy fur ball on my face, I decided I needed a visit to Cenk, the Turkish barber across the road from my lodgings. I trust Turks with hair more than any other nationality and Cenk—a butch, stocky Turkish elder originally from a Turkic minority group in Afghanistan—exuded an air of Zen masterery in the barbering craft. I felt completely at ease in his presence, more so than any doctor I'd been seen by at the ward or any professor I'd been lectured by at university. This guy was the real deal who commanded the respect of his junior barbers. I trusted him. Though a bit abrasive at first, if you persevere with him, talk to him a bit about his motherland and enjoy the one-on-the-house cup of grainy rocket fuel they call Turkish coffee (with a square of rose-scented candy), then you can kick back and allow the master to work his assortment of sinister-looking cut-throat razors and fresh-smelling aftershave balms and colognes on you.

I seemed to get on with foreigners, or could at least communicate with them much more fluently than I was able to with my own countryfolk. Perhaps it was because I was a bit like them: an outsider not in tune with the cultural norms, the language and the food of the host population. Ethnic enclaves in big cities, like New Malden (London's unofficial Koreatown) and Gröpelingen (a mini-Istanbul-come-Tehran in the western suburbs of Bremen), were the sort of places to which I instinctively gravitated. It was in those places you could find the good stuff, including the best food cooked from the home kitchens of the immigrant populations. And for a good price. They were devoid of pretence and artifice. They weren't watered down or pandering to a broad public. Fundamentally, they were honest places and I identified with them. Moreover, I could feel a connection to others through a shared love of their cuisine and through my own inquisitive childlike zest for experiencing their culture.

This same attitude of mine extended when I got back to the house from the barbers and came across my Spanish housemate, Andoni. He was a native of Bilbao and a proud exponent of all things Basque (though reassuringly he denounced ETA and any militant nationalist movements and violent terrorist groups like them). Like me, he put his faith in simpler things such as food. And, upon my arrival, I found him in our cramped postage stamp of a kitchen, which he appeared to permanently inhabit, where he was whipping up the best-smelling assortment of tapas in the rustiest frying pan on the grimiest hob known to man. The way he wrought simple ingredients into magic submission like that was pretty awesome—another master at work in the same square kilometre of this unremarkable German suburb. As I entered the kitchen I asked Andoni, who was infinitely personable, how he made his food taste so good. He replied: lots of olive oil and lots of garlic—six cloves, no less. I hope he wasn't kissing anyone that night. But given what was planned, he probably was. Quite a few people in fact.

That evening, on the very same day I'd just arrived from a stay in a mental hospital and wanted nothing more than to retreat into another bubble, there was to be a house party at *Bodelschwingstrasse*. From what Andoni was saying, the entire expat community in Bremen was invited. I didn't resent it, but the prospect of it terrified me, especially in my fatigued, nervous and highly-strung state. It seemed mean-spirited not to accept the olive branch offered to me, but I truly dreaded large gatherings, even at the best of times. They made me acutely aware of my sense of otherness.

While I could relate very comfortably to someone—even as extroverted and confident as Andoni—on a one-to-one basis, groups of people intimidated me beyond words. I had a deep aversion to such scenarios where binge drinking, inane chatter and loud music were the order of the day. I was having panic attacks to boot, which were becoming more and more frequent on quitting citalopram. While parties to most sane people in their early twenties are what one can actually look forward to, where one can let off some steam and not give a damn what anyone really thinks, to me they were a minefield of anxiety-inducing scenarios that threatened to expose my awkward disposition, my lack of concentration during moments of idle chatter, and my inability to cope with the sensory overload of being in a room full of music and people.

The non-stop multilingual chatter, the thumping bass, the blaring synths, the clinking of Becks bottles, the sight of couples making out, grown adults in fluorescent face paint, men in tutus, beads of sweat forming on people's foreheads, the lingering smell of BO and spilt Jägermeister all seemed too much. Such an amount of information was sure to tip me over the edge and provoke the mother lode of all panic. I'm inadequate to the task of describing just how scary it all seemed to me.

Anxiety is a weird thing. The dread of anticipating a panic attack can, somewhat ironically, cause a panic attack. Fear is so irrational it eventually ends up just being merely a fear of fear itself, or *angst vor angst* as the Germans would say. The fear of drowning in a sea of gregarious drunken revellers quickened my heartbeat. The physical symptoms of anxiety, though completely harmless, can be the most alarming. And minds like mine that are prone to catastrophizing often jump to the woefully illogical conclusion that something as benign as a twinge in the chest must mean that a heart attack is imminent, or a feeling of light-headedness must be the forerunner to a brain haemorrhage. The panic-prone mind plays tricks, devilish ones, that only perpetuate the vicious cycle of outright fear, followed by withdrawal, avoidance and deep depression. This merely compounds your feeling of worthlessness as a human being and forces you into a mindset that makes routine bonhomie impossible.

In my case, I'd gone into fight-or-flight mode at the very mention of the party. A few hours before it had even begun, I'd thrown a few scrunched-up items of clothing into a holdall, and discarded a few pristine unread university textbooks into the same plastic bag I'd thrown the months-old apple juice cartoons, paprika chip packets, salami wrappers and Krombacher cans (dregs and all). I went online and had soon printed off a Ryanair boarding pass bound for London Stansted Airport. My mission was to go under the radar of everybody and sneak back to Blighty without a soul knowing. Uwe wasn't going to be happy, but I doubt anyone who didn't want to hound me for money was going to kick up much of a fuss. After all nobody, not even the few pals I talked to a bit before my breakdown, came to visit me in the psych-ward.

7. THE BEAUTIFUL SURREALITY OF AIRPORTS

BREMEN AIRPORT AT 7PM. There was a hazy glow over the runway and the orange sun was beginning to set over the horizon. I was heading home and was due to arrive back in the UK late at night (my flight wasn't until 10pm). Apart from a tacky gift shop selling the usual range of half-arsed tourist souvenirs, there was quite an inviting, and strangely homely, bar and café in the departures lounge. It sold schnitzel rolls and wheat beer in tall litre-glasses, which is exactly what my rumbling stomach fancied. Perhaps it would soothe those frazzled nerves a bit. I ordered both and sat at one of the stools next to the viewing gallery overlooking the runway.

I love airports. They are surreal timeless places in which one feels extricated from the constraints of space and time—whatever life outside, whether successful or calamitous like mine—offering a kind of vague abstraction.

Just as I was about to tuck into my juicy behemoth of breaded pork in bread, a fat stinky traveller in glasses sat next to me. He was Canadian, I think, at least that's what I gathered when he asked me: *What's that book you're reading aboot?* It was actually quite an amusing survival guide for expats in Germany and it had invariably been my companion wherever I'd been, whether at the sausage vendor or in the mental hospital. German idiosyncrasies and foibles had to be laughed at or you simply couldn't survive there. The Canadian guy, it turned out (though I really, really wasn't in the mood to talk to him), just needed a drinking pal for the couple of hours he had to kill before his flight to the medieval city of Gdansk (next stop on his embarrassing cliché of a Eurotrip). Having overestimated the size of Bremen and the airport termi-nal, which was really just a shack with a bar, he'd arrived way in advance of his flight.

Usually I would have been pretty awkward around an English-speaking stranger I'd just met. But given the circumstances that had led me to this strangely trag-ic encounter between two diametrically-opposed hu-man beings, I adopted a more devil-may-care attitude to whatever this latest encounter was about to throw at me. I downed my first litre of the Bavarian nectar with consummate ease, reinforcing the negative stereotype this Canadian guy had of the borderline alcoholic, binge drinking Brit. He now felt compelled to keep up with me and did the same. I ordered another. He then ordered another. And the cycle repeated itself. You get the picture. The first two glasses gave us both mild blissful grins. By the third I was starting to slur my words. After the fourth glass, a mild depression seeped in and manifested itself in a dreadfully mawkish conversation about what a trial life can be. To the starched-shirted, pinstriped German businessmen around us in the café, we must have seemed like two overly expressive Anglophonic barbarians. But in that moment, I couldn't have cared less. I thought about mentioning the whole cannabis debacle to my new poutine-munching, igloo-building best friend, but thankfully still had the sense not to.

After several hours drinking, I stumbled onto the sardine tin that is a Ryanair plane. On the steps to the plane, I did my best to appear normal but became so self-conscious I seemingly forgot where I was putting my feet and ended up tripping over myself like a ruddy idiot. A very vigilant stern-looking German in severe rimless glasses picked me up, and two heavily perfumed and pretty Irish stewardesses then proceeded to guide me to my seat. How embarrassing. I was reprising my role as the famous bumbling stoned lunatic in Holland. My face blushed fiercely with shame as I reflected on how seemingly desperate my situation had become, how badly I was fucking things up, how my life was being blighted everyday by evil brutal bouts of panic and that all-consuming depression that just wouldn't lift. Not to mention I was blundering severely through every aspect of life, hopping like a startled hare on a busy country lane from one erratic decision to the next, with neither foresight nor the faintest regard for how my actions were impacting on others. And they were. Big time.

My jaded father greeted me at Stansted. He'd seen it once before when I'd run away in my Fiat Punto as a teenager before the start of a physics exam I was woefully unprepared for. He'd found me in a car park in Peterborough of all places. I had a habit of doing stupid things. He is so level-headed—perhaps the most even-tempered person on this earth—and there he was, displaying not even a trace of anger towards me. His face exuded a wounded disappointment though. He just didn't have any idea how to improve things for his son and had been so perplexed by what had happened in Holland and Germany, he really couldn't suggest anything. He was a rock though and forever the pragmatist who was there to pick up the pieces. He was the one who'd contacted the insurance company to pay for my stay in Germany and he was the one who got in touch with my university. He really was a saint. And so was my long-suffering mum.

8. NEXT STOP: LOSERVILLE

MY POOR PARENTS. They were the real victims of my self-destructive behaviour. And yet, they didn't once get angry with me. Perhaps they were too hurt or upset to do so. I was also a 24-year-old man, not a child, so scolding me like an infant wouldn't have been appropriate. Mum, though with a heavy heart, greeted me warmly at the doorstep of our family home. She'd had sleepless nights worrying about me in hospital and looked tired. It hurt me to see her like this. She'd prepared a homemade lasagne—my favourite. It was a labour of love for her. She'd spend hours preparing the sauce and pasta from scratch. It gives her pleasure to give. She lives to make others happy. Ultimately, she was just pleased to see her son in one piece. At least I was alive. At least I'd survived a psychiatric ward with all my faculties intact.

We sat at the family table, consciously ignoring the big elephant in the room of my stay in a German psych-ward. My parents were too weary to probe and I too weary to talk. We simply sat together enjoying the simple pleasure of a meal and being together at the dinner table. Our cat Smokey, an oddly intuitive little animal, somehow knew something was amiss. He seemed perturbed by our palpably strained conversation and the lingering feeling of sadness enveloping us all.

My parents are true saints. I know I keep banging on about it, but they truly are. They'd endured the hardship of having not one, but two autistic children. Me, the high-functioning, academically-gifted social misfit who was becoming increasingly prone to social meltdown. And my angelic little brother, Jack, who is non-verbal and, unlike me, severely handicapped. Jack wasn't the problem though. He is invariably the happiest of the two autistic siblings, adored by everyone with who he come into contact. His face is one of pure innocence. He has never spent a day worrying, fretting or panicking about a thing. He is a great leveller who has the ability to dissolve one's petty fears with his beautiful smile.

Mum and dad had fought tooth-and-nail to get him the right schooling he needed in the face of nightmarish bureaucracy and reams of red tape. They were used to fighting spirited battles without recourse to cynicism or hopelessness. They fought to the bitter end. But I was wearing on them. I just couldn't get it together and this latest episode had completely knocked the wind out of their sails. It was a sad state of affairs; the one functioning son, who had the ability to provide a ray of hope to his long-struggling parents was becoming an abject waste of space.

The bitch-goddess depression compounded my sense of guilt and that night I lay in bed and wept. The only thing that got me through it was the thought of Oliver and the kindness he'd showed me the time I had that panic attack. Despite my aversion to close contact, I had actually enjoyed his embrace the time we parted ways from Station 61 and could feel it again as I drifted into that pleasant state between asleep and awake. I wondered what he was up to and tried to picture his new flat. I wondered whether he'd smartened himself up, whether he'd kept shaving, whether he'd applied for a job. I doubted it though. That guy was on a downward spiral. I imagined him going back down the degenerate druggie route, mixing some rare strand of Afghani haze or opium he'd procured from a local gang of Kurds with the stash of Valium he'd nicked from the hospital.

On that thought alone, I refused to wax poetic about our friendship any more. It was nice while it lasted but it was over. He now served as the archetype of what I had to avoid becoming. I vowed, for the sake of my parents and for the sake of Jack, to hop off that non-stop express train to Loserville and find success in life.

9. HARD-GRAFT THERAPY

FIRST THINGS FIRST. I had to get myself fit. The combination of hospital inactivity, antidepressants and carb-heavy German food had made me kind of fat and listless. I was breathing heavily just walking up the stairs. I had a fair bit of time before the semester started that year back in Nottingham, so I decided that getting myself physically tip-top was the first step towards getting my head straight. I figured a few months of cycling around my native Essex, filling my lungs with the country air, slimming down, toning up and releasing some feel-good endorphins into my veins would do me the world of good, for sure. Before long, I thought, Bremen would seem like a distant memory I could laugh away over a pint at the local.

I got a job at the same place I'd worked consecutive summer holidays as a teenager at school. It was a kennels, a canine holiday camp, where dogs enjoyed the company of other dogs while their owners sunned themselves in Marbella or Sorrento. I loved it. It was honest physical toil in the resplendent beauty of the summer sunshine. This proved to be the best therapy so far for my low mood and anxiety, better than anything the so-called experts in the human psyche had offered me, and a thousand million times more useful than those bullshit qigong classes they were probably still doing in that grey utilitarian hospital building back in Bremen. Plus the dogs were fantastic company, better than that of a human being by far.

That summer was great. Memorable even. Despite still struggling with residual tiredness (getting up in the mornings was a real effort at times), the natural healing power of the summer sunshine vanquished those feelings the moment I stepped out of the house and felt the soothing wind on my face as I pedalled through the winding, sun-dappled country lanes on my bike passing fields of rape, wheat and barley en route to work.

Work was great. It didn't require me to make small talk with colleagues in a stifling office, grovel to superiors (I especially hated that shit) or deal with picky small-minded members of the general public. It was the same thing everyday: scooping up dog shit—some runny, as in the case of the perpetually shaking poodles and Bichon Frises, some in voluminous piles made by the larger more robust Rhodesian Ridgebacks and Great Danes—then disinfecting and squeegeeing the kennels. It may not sound fun, but it was infinitely preferable to working in a supermarket. I loved it. The endless routine, the lack of pretence and the graft. Then there was the feeling of humility that I was in no way above doing such a dirty job—one that would probably be considered the work of untouchable castes in certain countries. Cycling six miles to work everyday there and back got me fit, as did drinking gallons of cold Evian, eating freshly-prepared meals every day courtesy of mum (the days of paprika chips and Becks were long gone). Everything was doing me good. What's more, I had been panic-free for months now. Feelings of anxiety had become alien to my experience.

That was, until the rude arrival of term time. The summer had flown by, far too quickly in fact, and it was now time to start preparing for the upcoming semester. I made a vain half-hearted attempt to get ahead on my reading for what promised to be a gruelling final year replete with essay deadlines, endless reading lists and exams. I wasn't looking forward to this. My dad told me reassuringly to take things in my stride and that there was no pressure on me, as long as I tried my best. Despite feeling anxious about it all, I tried to stay positive.

10. A CLEMENTS NEVER GIVES IN

CRUISING ALONG THE M1 northbound towards Nottingham, my beaming father and long-time chauffeur was evidently in high spirits. He was ever the optimist and was proud that I was at least attempting to resolve things. *A Clements never gives in* is his beautifully pithy and uncomplicated motto to which he's adhered admirably in the many testing times he has encountered in his life. I, on the other hand, have given in to bouts of crippling self-doubt and despair all too easily. I am the opposite of him in many ways, and I was shitting myself about re-attending university after such a long absence.

However, I vowed not to let things get the better of me and to get a support network in place at the university to prevent a relapse of depression, or to at least give me the tools to deal with it rationally and calmly. We'd talked it through prior to the journey. I was to check in with my personal tutor regularly and not become isolated. I was also to book an appointment with the university's counselling service and seek the help of a warm-hearted and sympathetic counsellor (at least in theory). My dad forever maintained his faith that I had it in me to overcome my demons, my crippling shyness, my awkwardness and my lack of self-esteem. He desperately wanted me to be one of the lads. I wanted to be one too. If only I knew how.

Upon arrival at the accommodation, a newly-built complex with a clinical feel and a weird chemical smell in the corridors, I felt a sudden unexpected pang of homesickness. This was followed by an odd fluttering sensation in my chest. After such a blissfully peaceful summer holiday in the idyllic simplicity of the Essex countryside, it felt like I was now being summoned for war in a hostile environment, with lots of potentially lethal social minefields. Soon I would be forced to say hello and exchange inexplicably dire conversation with my new flatmates. Soon they would be inviting the inhabitants of the neighbouring flats in for a party that I had no way of escaping, bar putting on a pair of ear defenders and adopting a foetal position until it was all over. Hell, I dreaded everything about university, especially having to face those on my course.

Sure enough, during our year abroad debrief, the near-hysterical gossip about people's "amazing", "life-changing", "awesome" experiences in Germany was unbearably cringeworthy. Mine had been life-changing too, just not in the same way as theirs. People around me were bragging, in their jarring middle-class drawls, about seeing the Berlin Wall, the cathedral in Cologne, Neuschwanstein Castle, the Black Forest and Hitler's bunker—the common reference points of German culture, and the sorts of places you could just as well travel to by flicking through a Lonely Planet guide. I, on the other hand, had taken the less well-trodden path. I had been an intrepid dark tourist, preferring to see a cross-section of German society from the inside of a mental hospital. When somebody asked how Bremen had been, I told him: *Yeah, it was cool.* No more than that. I wasn't prepared to divulge anything more. I still cared about face.

People at the debriefing session were also keen to show off their German, which had no doubt improved after spending a year in the country. This was one thing I was confident about. Although I could barely hold a basic conversation with a stranger in English about the weather or the football without clamming up, stuttering and my face turning tomato red, I could quite happily natter for hours in a foreign tongue—whether German, French or Japanese. I was cocky about it too. It gave me, in my mind at least, a genuine sense of intellectual superiority and justified my aloofness, which in reality was a symptom of wretched self-esteem. Somehow, I'd unlocked in some deep recess of my brain that part that facilitates language learning. My mind was like a sponge mopping up vast amounts of vocabulary with an apparent lack of effort, while others wrote and revised endless vocab lists and practised cumbersome grammar exercises. I wasn't as clever as Dustin Hoffman's *Rain Man*, but I was damn close to being so.

Despite my intellectual prowess, my degree course held little appeal to me. I began to loathe what I saw as nothing more than a series of academic hurdles to leap over before the ceremony: with the silly archaic graduation gowns, and presentation of a piece of paper that parents and employers seemed to idolise. To tell the truth, I hated it.

My two new flatmates compounded my misery there. They were loud, uncouth, binge-drinking, absurdly self-confident, middle-class rich kids who coasted through their degree courses doing the bare minimum to meet the requirements for passing. I had zero in common with them. One was an over-privileged, privately-educated Bangladeshi with an American accent (though he hadn't spent a second in the States). He'd come to Nottingham for the nightlife, the uncivilised binge-drinking culture, the blonde women in mini-skirts and the daily promise of promiscuous sex with loose white women. He made me sick. I wanted to punch him for being such an objectionable twat. The other guy was just as bad. A stereotypical, jumped-up Hooray Henry, parodied countless times in various comedy sketches, who'd been raised by his French nanny while mummy rode horses and daddy went on business trips to Hong Kong. Fuck me, this sucked big time. Still I had to grin and bear it. And for a while I actually did.

11. A PASSAGE TO INDIA (VIA LEICESTER)

I DID WHAT I WAS SUPPOSED to for a while. I toed the line, read the books I was supposed to, went to (most) lectures—even a few of those pesky nine-in-the-morning ones—wrote assignments and even got them in on time. But things were eating me up again. My fitness from the summer was fading and so was my capacity for constructive thought. Slowly and insidiously, the depression crept up on me again. The voices telling me that life was beyond me grew louder. The self-doubt weaved its way into the fabric of my being and the panic attacks started. I could scarcely believe one person could have such rotten luck. The resolve I'd summoned, the Confucian sense of familial duty I'd adopted, and the vow to make my long-suffering parents proud of me once more were slipping between my fingers. Before long, I was skipping the odd class. The odd class soon became every class. And as for those counselling sessions—I'd quit after the first one. The limp, insipid lady with a silly high-pitched voice inspired little confidence in me.

Once again, like a recurring nightmare from childhood, I'd descended into a pit of self-destructive selfishness. Bags of pretzels had now become tubes of Pringles, while Dr. Pepper and Yazoo had now replaced apple juice and Becks. I began binge eating to mask the anguish. Tubs of choc-chip Haagen Daz were polished off, tikka masalas decimated and twelve-inch meat-feast pizzas were obliterated (their leftover boxes and errant crusts hung around for months in my slowly putrefying little room). Blocking out the sunshine with clothes on hangers, ignoring phone calls from family members, going out in public only to buy food, and whiling away my hours YouTube surfing had become my routine. It was eerily reminiscent of Bremen and I'd failed to act on the warning signs.

Several weeks passed. Several assignments had been missed. But by that stage I couldn't care less, I just wanted to remain in a fantasy. But believe it or not, I was tired and exhausted by doing nothing all day. So I decided to go walking. And I kept on walking. Four miles a day initially, from where I was living to Nottingham city centre. Before long, I broke into a run. I began imitating Tolstoy, one of my favourite authors, and became an exercise freak. I did everything in life with characteristic immoderation once I'd mustered the willpower to dive in head first. Things that started out as hobbies often became my sole focus, my raison d'etre, to the detriment of nearly everything else. I shed weight rapidly. I was disappearing before everyone's eyes. My alarm was set for 5am and by 6am I was out. Come rain, sleet, hurricanes or tsunamis, I was out there pounding the pavements of Beeston, Radford and Lenton. I ran five miles each morning and didn't deviate.

I also smartened up my look (I had a reputation for being a scruffbag), maintained an immaculate outward appearance, and adopted the look of a preppy PhD student—with a white shirt, blue woolly jumper, beige chinos and Clarks leather shoes. It belied a troubled, wrought-up, angry and depressed soul in need of set patterns and control in a chaotic incomprehensible universe. And yet I took pride in it, not least because it pleased my ever-concerned parents when they saw me during our weekly Skype conversation. It at least looked as though I was prospering in university life, even if the reality couldn't have been further from the truth.

After morning exercise, I'd always prepare a vegetarian meal. Following Tolstoy's example, I abstained from meat and animal products in search of some elusive spiritual enlightenment that would naturally fit my Spartan-like diet and fitness regimen. Vegetarianism was something I'd long flirted with but never had the guts to really embrace as a lifestyle. My parents were both veggies but had never foisted their alternative lifestyle on either of their two sons, thankfully. At heart I was an inveterate carnivore and, like my idol Anthony Bourdain, I loved eating every part of the animal, including the 'nasty bits' of offal: the hooves, the snouts, the lungs, the intestines—the unfashionable bits only Chinese peasants and my grandma still liked to eat. Despite going veggie (the label is still something I'm uncomfortable with), I refused to eat hipster food: hummus and mung bean burritos made by tetchy white feminists with dreadlocks. No thanks. It had to be authentic vegetarian cuisine I was eating. And which culture had the most ancient, established, tried-and-tested veggie cooking culture on earth? India. And where was there a large Indian enclave? Why Leicester, of course, somewhere that was just down the road from me.

It was my next mission, my new purpose in life, to find the apotheosis of vegetarian cooking on Leicester's Golden Mile: a two-mile stretch of curry houses, sweet vendors and saree shops. With childlike enthusiasm, I made the short trip south to where all the good stuff was to be had. Barely able to contain my excitement, I tried everything: pakoras, kachoris, khandvi, undhiyu, chaats, thalis, lassis, kulfis. I practically ate myself to ruin in the space of two short hours. After a final masala chai (which I was told would help digestion), I felt a twitch in my stomach. Rushing as far as I could from any oncoming pedestrians, I projectile vomited in a pedestrian subway by a busy overpass.

A benign and gentle little Indian lady dropped her two blue carrier bags containing fresh Asian vegetables, presumably for a home-cooked feast she was preparing for the family later that night, and came rushing to the rescue. The vomit kept coming. It was nasty. The Indian lady held me, patted me on the back and told me to let it all out in a calming tone. She reminded me in a split second of that blonde Dutch boy who'd called the ambulance and reassured me I wasn't going to die from a pot overdose in Holland. This lady really was an angel. I wished she was my grandmother and that she would take me back with her to nurse me with old Ayurvedic concoctions that had been passed down several hundred generations in her family. After a few deep breaths following the last of the vomit, she advised me with an irrepressible smile to drink some water and go home.

This time round no ambulances were required. I just skulked back to Leicester station and took the train back to Notts. I contemplated what the hell I was doing with my life on the lulling train ride through the flat East Midlands countryside. On the train, an elderly grey-haired gent with a ruddy complexion sat opposite me. Avoiding eye contact, I looked down at the floor to my shoes, then up to my chinos. They wore a huge vomit stain. I hadn't noticed it before. I almost died of embarrassment. Using my jacket, I concealed this dried congealed mess which was sure to stain and ruin my nice pair of trousers, especially given the amount of fluorescent yellow turmeric contained in the all the food I'd eaten. What a sorry individual I had become. Again.

Back in my room, I vowed—as I'd done countless times before—to sort out the mess I was in. I realised the physical exercise had only been a distraction from the real issue. But what was the real issue? I knew the answer to that but refused to look inwards for a solution. Instead I did everything to avoid facing up to my problems. I was too proud to admit I had, yet again, got myself into a dreadfully silly situation. So I bottled things up. I'd hidden them in the closet and under the bed. Facing up to the truth was difficult, but it was a necessity if I wanted to avoid yet another bombshell at home. The trouble was, I felt there was no one to turn to. I didn't believe even a counsellor—who'd more than likely seen far worse and heard stories far more heart-rending and tragic than mine—would understand or sympathise with the complexities of what I was experiencing. Even if they did, what would they offer in the way of solutions? Nothing most probably. Doctors were one potential avenue, but they'd only offer me another pill and that wasn't the answer. A serotonin cocktail or a noradrenaline pick-me-up would surely only mask symptoms, not cure them.

12. THE SHOPLIFTING INTERLUDE

I'M NOT SURE WHY I started shoplifting. Perhaps I was craving the sort of excitement that had been severely lacking in my life at the time, due to my inability to forge any meaningful connections with people. Perhaps it gave me a feeling of one-upmanship over the society I increasingly resented for rejecting me because of my oddness. Whatever the case, I actually don't regret doing it. For that brief time, when I was evading security staff and CCTV cameras, I felt truly alive. The rush I would feel when I made it out the door of whichever greedy and unscrupulous supermarket chain I robbed (I made a point of never stealing from small family stores) was unreal. I mean, like the best sensation on earth. What I imagine sex or the party drug ecstasy to be like.

The first time I stole, I concealed a chocolate bar in the sleeve of my coat and walked out, paranoid somebody had been watching me. The next time, I put a bag of almonds in each of my jacket pockets. This time I felt even more paranoid I'd been seen and even checked the local paper the next day for a CCTV still of me caught in the act. Then, as the anxiety waned, I progressed onto more expensive things like sashimi, parma ham, albacore and Bavarian wheat beer which I would shove into a carrier bag when nobody was looking. Eventually, as I grew in confidence and had virtually lost the fear of being spotted, I would walk into the shop brazenly with an empty rucksack and fill it to the brim with whatever I fancied. I must have gotten away with it a dozen times, feeling emboldened by each triumph. What's more, it felt brilliant to be in defiance of what I considered to be a rotten capitalist system (I, like most middle-class white kids, had their little lightweight Marxist left-wing phase). Rather than stealing these items, I convinced myself I was expropriating them from the rich corporations that had exploited the workers that produced them and divested the Earth of its resources in the process. I went so far as to believe I was on some sort of moral crusade, thinking it more moral to steal from such places than to actually give money to them.

This rather warped attitude changed in a small supermarket in the centre of town, a place that looked like a very innocuous and easy target. I was caught. Complacency had made me blind to a hawk-eyed security guard sitting by a monitor at the front of the store. I remember her vividly because she put the fear of God into me. She was a short, fat severe lady with a Jamaican accent and a take-no-shit Caribbean attitude. After nabbing a slab of parmesan and some sauce for a pasta dinner I'd planned that evening, I made for the exit of the shop and felt an arm pull me back in just as I was about to put my first foot out of the door. This lady was strong and fierce. I definitely wasn't going to mess with her. I reckon she'd watched me the entire time on her Orwellian telescreen. My heart pounded as she dragged me to the interrogation room out back, and my mind raced from one catastrophic outcome to the next. I'm going to jail. I'm going to have a criminal record. My life is ruined. I'm gonna get raped every night for two years by my heavily-tattooed cellmate.

When she'd finished dragging me to the back room, she pushed me unforgivingly into a chair and told me to wait. She left the room for a bit, presumably to discuss with the store's manager what punishment to inflict upon me. When she came back, she instructed me to empty my pockets and the contents of my bag. When I revealed the parmesan and the jar of tomato sauce, she seemed shocked and perhaps even a little disappointed. She must have thought she'd made the scoop of her career, but in reality the items I'd stolen barely amounted to £4 and were not enough to warrant a prosecution, let alone the bother of calling the police. *Is dat everyting?* she asked in her heavily lilted English. *Yes, everyting* I said, nervously imitating her accent but in no way intending to mock her. *OK, den, leave da shop reight now and never com back in 'ere. If ya do, I'll be waitin' for ya, you know.* The humourless security guard, whose livid eyes were now about to pop out of her enormous head, showed me the door and proceeded to give me one last disapproving shove as I exited.

I left the shop with both a feeling of relief and self-esteem that had been shattered into a thousand tiny fragments. Shoplifting had provided a means I could wrestle some control over a society that seemed relentlessly chaotic and nonsensical, but now that privilege had been taken away from me. I'm sure I could've gotten away with it elsewhere pretty easily, but risking a repeat of this fiasco seemed very unappealing. Despondent, I had to find another way of restoring some sort of order in my terribly dysfunctional life, and one that didn't involve risking arrest, a fine or worse a prison sentence and the sexual advances of a hairy, smelly and highly-testosteroned prison ape. The gravity of what I was doing only sank in when I arrived back at my student digs that evening and read an article in the Nottingham Post about a serial shoplifter in Newark who'd been monitored by police for months, finally caught and put behind bars for eighteen months. That could be me, I thought. I decided to stop stealing once and for all, not out of guilt or regret, but merely out of a fear of having to deal with the firm hand of authority.

13. NO MAN IS AN ISLAND, BUT SOME OF US ARE DROWNING

A BIG PROBLEM for autistics is that they are often left simply to fend for themselves. Alone in a wilderness of potential threats and predators. Lost in a sea of fear, confusion and disappointment. It's true that no man is an island, but a few of us in life—especially social outcasts—are often slowly drowning. At least, that's what it felt like for me. I had no mates to call for help. I had nobody in whom to confide. In my lowest moments I was essentially my own best friend. I wanted to connect with others around me, I really did, and yet I shielded myself with unrelenting cynicism and thoughts that were saturated in bitter resentment.

I had also begun to lie. A lot. A stereotype of autistic people is that we are remarkably honest, even when honesty isn't appropriate and white lies could have saved a lot of unnecessary bother. I too had been honest, to the point of rudeness at times. I had an awful habit of correcting people's bad grammar, spelling and punctuation; and I didn't hesitate to say how stupid they were if, God forbid, they used the wrong case or verb ending. On the other hand, during adolescence, I had discovered lying as a way of avoiding cross parents, irate teachers and stern authority figures. I'd now told so many lies to my parents it seemed impossible to extricate myself from the complex web of deceit I'd spun and in which I'd become irrevocably tangled.

I justified my lying because, ultimately, my biggest fear was hurting mum and dad. More than anything, they wanted to be proud parents attending my graduation ceremony with a framed photograph displayed proudly in a prominent position for every guest to see as they entered the living room. I truly believed a clichéd picture of me in ceremonial gown and mortar board, receiving a degree certificate from the college dean, was all they wanted. To be proud of their son for toeing the line and doing the right thing. And I was leading them to think they would be proud. It was inexcusable what I was doing. My immorality was flagrant and shameful. Though regardless of what predicament I was in, I still had the ability to tell right from wrong, and this was so blatantly wrong it makes me sick even writing about it.

The lies continued and were getting bigger and bigger. The bigger they were, the more convincing they seemed to be and the more confident I was of getting away with them. The biggest and most outrageous of them all came when the academic year was nearly over and my parents had received an email from the university. Oh, shit I thought, they'd finally told my parents I hadn't been present, that I'd ducked out of the whole year. But no! It was an invite to the graduation ceremony. I had to find a way out of this. An ingenious one. And it wasn't going to involve me being heroically honest either. Oh no, that ship had sailed long ago and wasn't making its way back any time soon.

As it happens, I stumbled on an unlikely way to avoid attending the ceremony and pretending to my parents I'd done the degree. It was to be the biggest hustle of the 21st century, but it wasn't one I was proud of. As far as I was concerned at the time however, it was absolutely necessary. I was doing this out of a twisted feeling of compassion. I didn't want my parents to suffer another blow because of my own ineptitude as a human being. I had to protect them from their abject failure of a son. And, for a while more, I did.

The plan involved a visa, a plane ticket and a lot of guts. In my endless hours of idleness, scouring the internet, Wikipedia page-hopping, YouTube-surfing, porn-watching and Facebook-stalking, I'd stumbled on a vacancy for a teaching job in China. It read succinctly: *Teach English at a private training school. No degree necessary. 7000 RMB a month. Free apartment.* It sounded suspiciously like a scam. But I didn't worry too much. Even if it was, it provided a get-out-of-jail-free card. I could use this job, whether it really existed in an actual school or in the basement of some organ-harvesting Triad gang, as an excuse not to have to attend my graduation ceremony—where I would receive a diploma, rather than the expected full degree, in front of heartbroken family members.

The next day, I hopped boxcars to Manchester Chinatown to apply for a visa. A few days later it arrived in the post. I booked my flight on Air China to the coastal city of Xiamen, previously known as Amoy to Westerners. I could scarcely believe I was fulfilling a childhood dream to see the Far East, one I'd long ago dismissed as something that could ever actually happen, even if I was doing so under the most unusual and frankly depressing of circumstances. Just as a child in the streets of Chinatown, I was again looking East to map an escape route out of my own personal hell.

All packed up and immunized from nasty tropical diseases, courtesy of a flying visit to the family home in Essex, I was leaving again. This time to a land that had hitherto only existed in my imagination, but one I seemed destined to see someday and experience first-hand. I just didn't realise it was going to be quite so soon. It had been a heavy burden deceiving my parents like this day in, day out, week after week, but somehow I'd survived. I had to. For their sake and for my own.

Dad, ever my chauffeur, drove me to Heathrow. I felt choked about saying goodbye and barely suppressed a flood of tears. How could I do this to my parents? After what they'd been through? After what I had promised? It's a wonder I didn't go insane, living this terrible lie.

The disorientating frenzy of departures, the heady perfume smells in the Duty Free shop, the strange mix of racial denominations downing pints of Guinness at the bar at a completely inappropriate hour of the day, the extensive book range at WH Smith, and my snack of utility supermarket sushi with a carrot smoothie thankfully gave me little time to think.

The thought of fulfilling a lifelong dream was tantalisingly close to being a reality. In fifteen hours I would be in China, an alternate reality where Nottingham, Bremen, my autistic habits, my anxieties and my tendency towards depression would all seem irrelevant. I'd soon be taking a nibble off the edge of a world filled with wonder. This vast land of mythical dragons, kung-fu, ancient incense-infused Taoist shrines, naff karaoke bars, opium dens and cavernous *dim sum* palaces would ordinarily have driven me out of my mind with the kind of excitement I'd experienced as a kid in Soho. But now, as a 24-year-old blowing every opportunity for self-advancement in life and deceiving my parents to boot, I just wasn't feeling it. At one stage, I even contemplated turning back.

The flight there was bad. I tried to summon enthusiasm by delving into the Lonely Planet guide mum had bought for me. But I couldn't concentrate on it. I was travelling to somewhere I'd long dreamed of but was in completely the wrong state of mind, encumbered with a heavy guilt that hung around my neck like an albatross for the fifteen hours I was hunched in cattle class. A marathon session of Mr. Bean followed by Porridge and two painfully average "thrillers" starring the ever-wooden Orlando Bloom (or Orloondo Bland as I prefer to call him), made for thoroughly unpleasant viewing. The Air China inflight meal provided about the only entertainment. A volcanically hot steaming tray of saggy chicken noodles and, to appease us flabby white folk, a bread roll and some butter. It was an incongruous combination and not one that I found particularly endearing. I ate about half and couldn't muster the rest.

After what seemed an eternity, I landed on terra firma, my ears enjoying relief from the incessant whir of the plane's engine. I was in Bangkok for a five hour stopover en route to Xiamen. I now felt pretty ecstatic about being in the Far East for the first time. Stepping off the plane, I was hit immediately by warm tropical air and smoky aviation fumes. It just didn't feel right though. My heart was pounding on the shuttle bus en route to the terminal. Lack of sleep wasn't helping suppress the demons that were alarmingly rising to the surface. I was sure the earth was going to swallow me up. Depression, panic and now a vast terminal filled with passengers. The omnipresent relentless heat and humidity didn't help either.

In a moment reminiscent of the cannabis incident Holland, I collapsed onto a hard seat in the waiting area of the departures lounge, doing absolutely everything in my power to suppress a flood of tears whilst keeping a lid on the whirlpool of afflictive emotions (including guilt, sadness, anxiety, despair, emptiness and absolute lack of hope). I was surrounded by a sea of people, a cross-section of humanity, who remained hopelessly unaware of what I was feeling. Intense loneliness was next. I was all alone, on the other side of the world, without a soul to confide in. East Asians, whom I considered model stoics and pragmatists, would most likely see me as yet another inward-looking, overly-emotional random whitey. They weren't gonna help me if I was in trouble.

After a brief respite, I pulled myself together and ordered a bowl of ramen from a trendy, pseudo-Japanese fast-food joint. I got the one with pork belly and a gratuitous fried egg on top. The little fat globules floated to the surface of the rich meaty broth. It really calmed me with its warm savoury flavour. This was the first time I'd eaten meat in a while and it was great. I felt better and stronger for it. One Vietnamese coffee later (if you haven't tried Vietnamese coffee by the way, do so, because it's the best coffee you'll ever drink in your life), and it was time to finish the final leg of this long-ass trek to China. Just as I had become relaxed and settled at the airport, it was time to leave again.

This flight was a culture shock in and of itself. For a start, I was the only white face on the plane. The rest were Chinese Mainlanders. You could tell they were Mainlanders because of their appallingly bad manners and their compulsive habit of spitting in the toilet sink. I don't just mean spitting, I mean hocking up loogies. It offended every British sensibility in my bones. Disgusting. Vile. Filthy. Where the hell was I headed? Were all Chinese going to be like this? Was this how modern Chinese actually behaved? The flight there was short and I actually managed to sleep for at least part of it. I even dreamed about Gerard Street and those Saturdays immersed in a culture distinct from my own that held so much allure for me. Was the real China going to be like this? I was nervous with anticipation.

I had arrived. I had made it to the land I'd dreamed of seeing since I was a young boy—even if I'd taken a highly unorthodox route to get here. A chap called Tam (real name unpronounceable) greeted me at the airport. He was a big guy, quite unlike the diminutive Southern Chinese I'd been accustomed to seeing in London. He had a bone-crushing handshake, a husky voice and an impressively awesome grasp of English. At this stage, I still wasn't sure if this was a scam or not, though to be honest I didn't even care.

Leaving the airport terminal, I was now entering into the alternate reality that is modern China. Gone are the days of daily commuting by bicycle. This was a land of big four-lane highways, tall high-rises and American-style shopping malls. I'd kind of been expecting this, and I still yearned to explore the rural hinterland, old parochial backwaters, bamboo houses, Buddhist shrines, and farmers in sampans. To my dismay, the first place Tam took me before embarking on the bullet train to the city of Longyan—where I was to teach for an entire year—was Starbucks. He treated me to what he considered to be a 'taste of home': a Starbucks coffee. I hate Starbucks. The coffee barely tastes like coffee. It's the lowest grade dreck you can buy. More milkshake vendor than coffee shop. Still, I appreciated the gesture. He ordered a luminous matcha green tea latte for himself (like many Chinese he found coffee unpalatable), whereas I just opted for a plain black Americano.

An hour later, after a short trip in the smelliest cab known to man, we boarded the train to Longyan, a place I was told there were no foreigners. Fuck; it dawned on me then that I was going to be truly on my own there. If I had a panic attack, there wasn't going to be a hospital to check into either. My cynical side told me instead that maybe a quack doctor could have a quick sniff of skin, examine the colour of my tongue, read my palm, stick needles in me and prescribe me a potion of assorted forest-floor sweepings that I would have to drink as a foul-tasting tea at regular intervals throughout the day. (In reality, China does have modern Western pharmacies, albeit with a mixture of traditional and frankly useless remedies for minor ailments.)

On a modern German-engineered train route that had only recently been built, we passed through the sprawl of urban Xiamen and scythed elegantly through the luscious green rice paddies, manicured tea plantations, and serene villages of Fujian Province. Traditional *erhu* music played on the train's sound system. It was a beautiful juxtaposition of the old and new China. It got me excited. This was the China I had hitherto only seen in books, on murals in the local *Peking Garden* restaurant, and on Michael Palin's *Around the World in 80 Days*. My mood lifted with a childish sense of wonder at the beautiful scenery and ethereal music. This was the beginning of a real adventure.

We arrived at Longyan (in English, the name translates as 'Dragon Eye' which seemed very evocative) a few hours later. The school's owner—a beautiful slender woman with soft olive skin and long, thick, silky black hair—greeted me. She was impressed by my self-taught Mandarin, and immediately remarked upon how handsome I was. I'd never considered myself particularly good-looking, I was average-looking at best, but in China—apparently—I looked like DiCaprio. I could certainly dig that. Blue eyes were a rarity here, and so I guess were white skin and light brown hair. It was a flattering compliment, if a little insincere.

As per Chinese custom, the school's owner, Michelle, invited her guest from afar to a restaurant. The Chinese are among the best in the world at hospitality. I was exhausted and frankly just wanted to pass out in my bedroom for a solid thirteen hours. But not wanting to offend my new hosts, I played the perfect guest. It was a veritable banquet, and she ordered more for me and Tam than we could possibly eat. The food was out-of-this-world. I mean, really, really good. It made the food I'd eaten in Gerard Street seem like a pale imitation of the sheer depth and diversity of native Chinese cooking. And this was just the beginning! I'd had but a tiny nibble off the edge of a vast country of over a billion people. A country which promised limitless possibilities to the bold journeymen such as myself. I knew I was going to like it here. I felt at home already.

I crashed out at my apartment on the 42nd floor of a huge concrete monstrosity. This was to be my home for the next twelve months and, to be honest, it was cosy. A Westerner may have baulked at the idea of sleeping on a hard mattress, as is typical in these parts, but I didn't mind. The apartment had a kitchen, a wok, a knife, an all-in-one toilet and shower, a bed, and a desk where I could compose my bestselling travelogue. It was simple, yet perfect for my needs.

The next day I awoke to a succession of loud bangs. What the hell? Turns out they were firecrackers, for good luck and to usher in prosperity for a newly-opened local business. China was my oyster for a few days before school started. This is how freedom tasted. I didn't care less about all my problems back home, they were irrelevant now I was here. I vowed to stay in the here and now, to enjoy every sense, sight, sound and smell around me—and to hopefully have a few epiphanies in the Middle Kingdom.

I could barely contain myself as I stepped out of my apartment into the dusty humid streets of my new neighbourhood. I had to try every item of street food and eat my way through the full spectrum of Chinese cuisine, observe every game of Mahjong, say *ni hao* to every passer-by who found themselves captivated by the tall, stubble-faced blue-eyed curio that was me. This, or so I am told, is called the honeymoon phase. It lasted a good two days before the reality of what was required of me reared its ugly head.

14. FAKING IT AS A TEACHER

I HADN'T SO MUCH been hired as a teacher, than as a white face for the company. But I kind of knew this already. I knew China was a culture pre-occupied with, and built on the cult of, face. I had no qualms about this either. Selling one's soul is a necessity of living in the global economic system.

The school was flash, modern and only recently built. It was one of many thousands across the country fuelling the English teaching boom. It was all artifice of course. The school was really a business, selling to nouveau riche Chinese—most from peasant-farmer stock who'd made a fortune selling their land to real estate developers and were now showing off their wealth and status. And I was the star attraction. More than anything, the materialistic Chinese loved to brag about their son and daughter being taught by a real-life, in-the-flesh white Westerner. My pale skin and blue eyes, not my teaching ability, were what the school wanted. And sure enough, the fanfare began the moment I stepped through the door of the shiny new school. Photos were taken of their high-ly-prized Caucasian zoo animal. Everybody wanted their picture taken with me. Most had never even seen a white person in the flesh. I'd gone from a loner in my bedroom to the centre of attention in a matter of days. It was a strange and frankly uneasy transition.

I wasn't good in photos. I couldn't fake a smile and I hated the flash. It always makes me wince and recoil involuntarily. But I had to do it. I took selfies with admiring colleagues, all of whom were petite women with cute smiles, posing with the stereotypically Asian peace signs. The head teacher, Ivy, was so pretty she made me blush. A country girl who'd grown up in one of the province's poor rural villages, she had an earthy dark complexion, a tiny mouth and a slim build. After the annoying photo session, Ivy introduced me to the school, the classrooms and a class of students. I was only the second foreign teacher they'd ever had at the school.

I was a valuable commodity. They went out of their way to take good care of me, to ensure I didn't do a famous midnight run (something a lot of disenchanted foreign teachers do in China, apparently). At that stage, the thought of jacking everything in seemed ludicrous. For the first time I felt welcomed, wanted, appreciated, liked, admired and attractive. The female attention, the first I'd ever consciously experienced in my life, went to my head a bit. But before I got carried away, the sobering thought that they were deliberately putting me on a pedestal and treating me like a god for the sake of their business reminded me to put on my serious face.

Ivy, with whom I ever so slightly fell in love at first sight, introduced me to a class of 5- to 7-year-olds, all of whom were obedient and looked visibly fatigued (probably from all the extra-curricular classes, piano lessons and dance tutorials they were forced to do by their overly-pushy and ambitious Chinese parents). You had to feel a bit sorry for them. But they were, undeniably, cute as buttons. Their collective adorableness as they sat on dinky little plastic chairs next to each other, some yawning and some with drooping eyelids, was extremely sweet. I loved them all at first sight. Anny, their strict lead teacher, barked commands at the weary children in a mixture of the local Fujianese dialect and Mandarin. She elicited almost immediate responses from the kids who had a strong sense of deference to authority, very alien to most kids in the West. These Chinese kids were ideal students. Or so I thought.

The next day as I took control of my first class, with no prior training, I had an entirely misplaced confidence that I could ace it and that this teaching malarkey would be a piece of cake. How wrong I proved to be. The obedient class I'd witnessed the night before were an exception. The kids this morning were young Chinese tearaways. Really naughty little emperors and empresses who were spoilt rotten by their rich materialistic parents. Unlike the Chinese teachers who still commanded respect even among the worst-behaved kids, I was nothing but a source of amusement. An oversized European clown with hair on my arms and chest, enormous dinosaur feet (size 11 is significantly bigger than the average Chinese male's shoe size) and wacky blue eyes. Despite my grasp of Mandarin, which had become a little rusty by then, they did not respect me. It felt like most of the time my words were being sucked into a vacuum. My first class was an unmitigated disaster. The kids barely acknowledged my presence and instead proceeded to run around, in full view of their scrutinising parents who were watching on a creepy Orwellian telescreen outside. It was embarrassing to say the least. I really thought I could go in and teach a class of fifteen hyperactive kids without any prior preparation. The next class was equally disastrous. As were the subsequent seven that day.

I arrived home feeling like a political prisoner must feel after a day's torture. My self-esteem, that had momentarily skyrocketed after the numerous compliments I'd been given, had vanished below ground. My parents and I had agreed to talk on Skype that evening, but I made a phoney excuse I was going out with work colleagues that night. In addition to the teaching debacle, I was living on a permanent edge that my parents might know the truth about why I absconded to China. That I'd lied through my teeth for months and lacked the basic human decency to tell them what they deserved to know. My head felt like egg being been made into an omelette. It was too late to unscramble the mess it was in. I was irrevocably fucked.

The next day, I returned bravely to school. Everyone there was remarkably composed. I'd half expected to be censured by Ivy or the boss. But no. It was water off a Peking duck's back to these people. Turns out they didn't give a damn how badly I taught. As long as I spent forty five minutes at a time in the classroom with the kids whose parents were paying a monthly fee way above the average salary of ordinary working-class Chinese, it didn't matter. I might as well have been miming or talking absolute gibberish. The nouveau riche in China were so ludicrously superficial, they didn't care. They likely knew I wasn't trained, that I was an unqualified low life backpacker without a single ounce of credibility.

The real teaching was done the old-fashioned way, rote-style by the lead Chinese teachers. A lot of repetition was involved in their classes, as though they were bashing vocabulary into the children's minds with a giant hammer. Creativity was considered mere folly. The lead teachers did all the work, marked the children's exercise books, set homework assignments and maintained an order and discipline impossible for me, the hapless foreign ape, to maintain. Despite this, I was on a salary near three times theirs'. I couldn't sit easily with this gaping inequality and upon learning of it I felt sick.

Notwithstanding the hellish grief and worry I'd put my parents through, it reassured me to know I still had the remnants of a conscience in me. I hated the setup. I hated being put on a pedestal, being fawned on and treated like someone special. I wasn't special in the slightest. I'd done nothing—zilch—to deserve the honour. While I wasn't completely against selling my soul, it just seemed wrong having these poor but exceedingly bright and well-educated young Chinese ladies doing all the dirty work while I was the one having all the attention ladled on me. Though I had no other option right now—consistency was something I craved, despite being in the midst of this unusual moral dilemma. I had to persevere with this job. It had at least landed me in China, a place I was still keen to throw myself head first into given the first possible opportunity. And this I did.

My first trip was to the *tulou* buildings, distinctive round communal fortresses built out of earth by the persecuted Hakka minority. The highlight of that trip was being invited to a home-cooked lunch by an elderly Chinese couple living close by. She cooked a veritable feast of local delicacies including beef meatballs, soup noodles and a plethora of stir-fried green vegetables all washed down with crisp, delicious green tea grown in the surrounding mountains. It was one of the loveliest most peaceful meals I'd ever had. The warmth showed by the couple really touched my heart. We laughed heartily, drunk tea till it was coming out of ears, and ate more food than a Tang dynasty army. I felt, for the first time, so relaxed that I was gutted when it was time to leave.

Meanwhile, teaching at the school went from bad to worse. Moreover, they were piling more classes onto me. By now, at least, I was actually planning things a bit and trying to win the kids over. Deliberately playing the clown worked and humour, especially of the slapstick variety (something I wasn't naturally gifted with), appealed to the kids and made them listen to what I was saying. But it all became too much for me. The big classes, the gossipy parents outside in reception watching me, and the feeling of being a mere novelty to these people were all wearing on me.

Maybe I'm too thin-skinned or overly philosophical, but I knew after three months of faking it as a teacher in front of largely disinterested kids in a Chinese backwater (which, despite all the good food, I wasn't especially fond of), I had to up and leave. Early morning, in the midst of monsoon season, I boarded a sleeper train to Hong Kong. It was a spontaneous decision, and one by that time I had little regret in making.

15. TRAGIC TRANSIENCE

THE HONG KONG-BOUND TRAIN wasn't like the flashy bullet train I'd taken from Xiamen. This was slow and provincial. And so were the people on board—leathery, sun-beaten migrants and peasants from the rural south. Using Mandarin with them was useless. They were uneducated toothless simpletons who only spoke in rough choppy dialects that were unintelligible to many of their fellow Chinese, never mind outsiders like me. Away from the high-rises and shopping malls this was the real China, the way 60% of Chinese (around 750 million) still lived in grinding poverty, eking out a living by labouring under the auspices of unscrupulous and exploitative contractors.

I shared a carriage with three chain-smoking men in leather hats. They were brutally ugly but friendly, and not in the least bit hostile to the unexpected intrusion of a foreign devil or *gweilo* (literally 'ghost' as they say in Cantonese). For eighteen very long hours, we chugged along at nearly a crawl on our conspicuously low-tech locomotive through wet luscious fields of bamboo, over fast-moving silt-infused rivers and through dense sub-tropical woodland. I arrived in Shenzhen, on the border with Hong Kong, at three in the morning. The only two places open were a 7-Eleven store and a KFC. I went to both, eating confectionery I'd bought as a kid in Gerard Street at the Chinese supermarket—things like VLT Lemon Tea, Pocky chocolate sticks, green tea Kit-Kats and wasabi peas. I again felt like the child in London's Chinatown ten years previously.

I sat in a drab and dingy little KFC waiting for the Hong Kong border to open at 6am. Before me was a rather manky Chinese breakfast of *pi dan shou rou zhou*, a rice porridge with black ammonia-preserved eggs and air-dried pork. Yum. The natives of Shenzhen, a city on the edge of the mainland that now dwarfs Hong Kong in terms of size and population, were evidently used to seeing foreigners. They weren't staring at me and it was liberating to be anonymous again.

As 6am approached, a crowd gathered by the entrance to Hong Kong before the sluice gates opened. After a long walk through various checkpoints and unnecessarily long-winded officialdom, I'd reached the subway in Hong Kong. Names like Mong Kok, Kowloon and Tsim Sha Tsui all sounded so familiar. This was the China I'd grown up with—way before I'd sought the real stuff in Chinatown—when all I knew of anything Chinese were Western-friendly classics such as electric pink sweet and sour pork, the greasy spring roll and the gloopy wanton soup. They'd all been cooked by immigrants from this tiny densely-packed patch of land that immediately had an energy, a feel, a vibe and an attitude very distinct from the Mainland. It was my kind of place and the possibility to eat superb food was just a short subway ride away.

When I got to Mong Kok, I cut loose and decided to wing it. While most headed for the Victoria Peak tram or to see the Golden Buddha, I followed my nose through the chaotic street markets with live eels and clams shooting water at passers-by, the rabbit warren of grubby roadside noodle joints, the modern shopping districts with air-conditioned pedestrian overpasses, and the kaleidoscopic array of food stalls and places to eat *dim sum*. Whatever there was, I was gonna eat it all up greedily and voraciously. The thrill was indescribable. Having the freedom to be in a place where every square mile is densely packed with all the things I love made me ecstatic. If there's anything close to heaven on earth for me, this must surely be it.

I must have covered about twenty miles on foot that day; what most visitors would cover in five days I'd managed in just one. But as night fell and the magnificent harbour was lit up by a stunning multi-coloured light display, I realised I had to find a place to stay. As per my typically short-sighted habit of rarely planning anything sensible, I hadn't booked myself in anywhere or even bothered to research a place. Thankfully in Wan Chai, a district on the Hong Kong side across the harbour from Kowloon, I found a hostel. Incidentally, they alleged that famous whistle-blower Ed Snowden had stayed there, but I didn't believe them. Initially I hated the idea of being in a hostel. I hated being in close proximity to strangers. I hated the inevitability of making small talk with a bunch of empty-headed, idealistic 20-something white backpackers on their gap years in Asia who wanted to find themselves. These fears were unfounded and the people in my room were some of the nicest and most beautifully eclectic group of people I'd ever met.

One guy was an aspiring travel writer from Seattle, en route to Mainland China where he was to meet up with his mother. Like a typical American traveller, he'd left no room for spontaneity and had every single day, hour and minute of his 4-week trip cramming in every conceivable landmark, museum and photo opportunity in the Middle Kingdom. It was exhausting just reading his itinerary. The other guy was a heavily tattooed French-Canadian chef from Montreal. I liked this guy a lot. Like me, we both liked food, and like me he was an avid fan of Bourdain.

Sharing my experiences with them over in the Mainland was great. Unlike people back home, they were genuinely interested in what I had to say and shared my enthusiasm for the allure of the East. As we got better acquainted, we cracked open a few cans of Tsingtao beer the previous nights' occupants had left in the communal fridge. We laughed and enjoyed ourselves, talking to each other of the grandiose plans we all had for the future. The aspiring writer wanted to open a chain of book-themed coffee shops (still not sure what he meant by that). The rock 'n' roll chef wanted to open a French bistro with an Asian twist, hence why he was scouring the continent for ideas which he jotted down in his little, beaten, sauce-stained leather-bound journal.

While we tarried at the hostel for a good hour or so, we were joined by a German girl who'd arrived back from Kunming. She was a neuroscientist by trade, but from her outward appearance she looked like a stereotypical white backpacker. She was sunburnt from all the high altitude mountain trekking and her pink skin was peeling. After another hour, we all ventured into Hong Kong, throwing ourselves into this giant, neon-lit pinball machine of a city with wanton abandon. That night we all lived in the moment and the happy randomness of it all was exhilarating.

After a meal at one of Hong Kong's funkiest *dim sum* spots we hit upon Wan Chai, where all the bars were, and went from one expat bar to the next. The Chinese weren't ones for nightlife that didn't involve an activity like karaoke or bowling, so this was a highly Western enclave nestled in the depths of this magical South China metropolis. After God knows how many pints of lager, which were sweated out rapidly in the sweltering heat outside, we headed to watch the light show over the magnificent Hong Kong harbour. This was a moment of sheer transcendence, where time stood still; I was in complete awe in a state of higher-consciousness. The sense of connectedness I felt to my three foreign comrades—whom I had only known for a mere drop in the ocean of life— was sublime. For the first time ever, I had an urge to hug these new friends and felt relieved from the burden of being myself.

The next morning however, it had dissolved into memory. The two guys had left before I woke up. The German girl had gone with a stranger from one of the bars. It was all over. I felt a gentle melancholy come over me as I contemplated the transient nature of good things in life—those rare fleeting moments one had to treasure in life because they were so few and far between. It dawned on me there and then that there wasn't enough good stuff happening in my life. I craved that connection and vowed to find it again.

For now though, staying in Hong Kong was proving very expensive. The money I'd earned in China didn't exactly go far here and, worried I'd overspend, I made the sensible choice to buy a ticket back home. I paid in cash at the airport with the leftover *renminbi* I had in my pocket. London was calling.

16. INTO THE WOODS

EVERYONE BACK HOME wanted to know about my Chinese adventure. While most of my Nottingham cohort had graduated (and most likely slotted in to some corporate office in Germany, signing their life away at the drop of biro ink to paper), I had done China on my own. I'd staked out a position as a daredevil traveller—braving squat toilets and gutter oil in the back of beyond, and taking trains that traversed vast swathes of the rural undeveloped south—and I'd lived to tell the tale.

I shared my tale exuberantly, with a quasi-philosophical air, romanticising about how China challenged my preconceived Western ideas and prejudices—all the while forgetting the real reason why I went there in the first place. Luckily my parents weren't enquiring as to why no degree certificate had arrived in the mail. This had always been a niggling worry in the back of mind, but thankfully they were too distracted by my saccharine descriptions of teaching sweet, obedient Chinese children, my Palinesque 18-hour train journey with a bunch of chain-smoking Cantonese labourers, and being truly grossed out by my lunches of duck feet and pig offal soup.

There wasn't any room at the inn for me though and really, at this age, I ought to have moved out of mum and dad's by now. But my money was sparse. I had no choice but to move in with my grandmother. Ninny, as I'd called her from a young age (I'm still clueless as to why exactly), isn't your typical cotton-head granny who knits itchy woollen jumpers and drinks tea from a pot all day. She's the sort who, even in her early eighties, still enjoys playing pranks on people and is always up for a drinking session. Her body—riddled with aches and pains brought about by arthritis, rheumatism and two replacement knees—could not keep up with her relentlessly curious mind and lust for adventure.

We got on like a house on fire and moving in with her was far from a burden on either of us. Our relationship was reciprocal: I cooked the dinner and kept the house clean, while she provided me with a free place to stay. This arrangement suited us both well. Moreover, we enjoyed each others' company and I related to her better than anyone in my own age group. Young autistic people often have a close relationship with their elder relatives; older people can be mellower, less judgmental, less uptight and more forgiving than their children. They are less wrapped up in self-image and many are beyond being bad-tempered and irascible.

Ninny was a kind lady whose Irish mother had bestowed upon her a big heart and the true gift of the gab.

She could talk for hours without pausing. It was fine by me because I enjoyed listening. To most distractible twenty-somethings she was a boring old fart, but to me she was an archive of London history, from the Blitz to the swinging sixties.

Reading way into the night, often until past three in the morning, she kept her mind sharp. Unlike her sister, Colleen, who was the more glamorous of the two sisters in their youth, Ninny had retained her faculties and never stopped learning. She even composed short stories which, while not especially highbrow, shone through with an endearing mix of Irish wit and East End charm. She'd published a few in national magazines. Despite her limited education, she loved words. She was a writer, but more to the point, a lover of literature by the likes of Dickens and Bronte.

Her warmth and affection towards others endeared her to everybody in the town where she lived, to the point every passer-by would stop and say hello to her. Even so, she wasn't everybody's friend and trusted very few. She preferred to remain a tough and proud individual, rather than join the shallow uncomprehending herds destined to rot in a nursing home having pureed food fed to them by abusive care staff. I respected her militant individualism and her refusal to grow old. I could imagine myself being like that at her age.

Often we'd make plans together of where we wanted to go. I'd pull out an old Times World Atlas she'd bought for me when I was young—a book that fuelled my irrepressible urge to see the world—and we'd plan an itinerary for an imaginary trip to India, say: starting in Amritsar and working our way along the Western Ghats until we reached the southernmost tip of the subcontinent at Cape Comorin. Occasionally we'd go to the local cinema and see a film we'd usually deplore as soppy American dross, or enjoy some tea and a bacon sandwich at the local café. After the comedown of returning to the grey oppressive skies of Blighty, enjoying life's simple pleasures with my grandmother was just what I needed.

My routine was simple and rhythmic—harmonious even. Each day began at 9am. My grandmother and I weren't early birds; we were both of the Oscar Wilde persuasion that only dull people are brilliant at breakfast. I'd get up, make her tea and bring it to her in bed. It took her several cups to 'bring her round' in the mornings. I'd tidy up the kitchen and spend a few hours reading books on Japanese and Korean cooking, ogling over pictures of marbled tuna at the Tsukiji fish market in Tokyo, and freshly prepared kimchee fermenting in earthenware pots in Busan. Indulging in all things Eastern, despite being back in the West, sustained me. Kept me alive even. Everybody needs a teddy bear to hug, and that was mine.

I'd go from the library to the coffee shop—a Portuguese one with a bright yellow display of cinnamon-dusted custard tarts—to get my twice-daily espresso fix. I'd missed good coffee in China. The only variety you could get there was a 3-in-1 powder made by Nescafe in some dusty corner of the supermarket that nobody, except maybe a homesick expat, would ever venture into. It didn't taste like coffee. I'm not even sure it had any coffee in it.

The Madeirans in my town were a sociable bunch and their homely little cafe was the hub of their little expat community. They didn't really want to be in Britain, and who could really blame them? They had everything good back home: sunshine, beautiful scenery, amazing food, a relaxed pace of life, music in the streets. Britain is a place everybody locks themselves behind doors, where we pay inflated prices for mediocre food in chain restaurants, and binge drink on a Friday evening instead of savouring a nice wine. The Madeirans were dynamic attractive people, too. They were slender and dusky; not the frumpy bison-sized lumps we've become in Britain. They didn't take work too seriously. They lived to eat, to spend time with their family, and enjoy a beer with garlic king prawns at lunch. I liked them and quickly found my niche in a town that was ever so slowly becoming a soulless homogenized strip of chain stores and pretentious coffee shops in which people sit for hours on a sofa with a latte (which British people inexplicably pronounce *lartay*). It felt like being in the Mediterranean and, like I'd done countless times before, I escaped in to a foreign alternate reality.

I also found an escape in literature and had begun reading Thoreau's *Walden*. His idea of the simple life was appealing. I thought emulating his example might just yield some sort of spiritual benefit—that by preserving my individuality, whilst merging with nature and the cosmos, I'd find enlightenment. His renunciation of the extraneous things and elements that sully our souls and his refining of life to its most essential appealed to me. His individualism and iconoclasm more so. He represented to me the ultimate rebel who refused to throw in with any religion or political ideology in order to discover the elusive *truth* we all seek.

His wooden rustic cabin in Walden woods in Massachusetts would not look out of place in feudal Japan, where organic asymmetry, moss and decay were prized over Western standards of precision and ostentation. Thoreau bridged an all-important gap between the cultural schisms of East and West, which is why I gravitated towards him. I too was torn between both worlds, but had failed to reconcile myself to either. Hell, I could barely reconcile the conflicting elements in myself.

I still wanted to make friends, but the Madeirans wouldn't have me. They were a cliquey bunch, abrasive towards outsiders and interlopers. I plucked up the courage to speak to one guy, an embittered postman who had a reputation for driving his mail van like a rally car, but he didn't want to know. Neither did the old guy in a flat cap. I wasn't one of them, and was never going to be.

So Thoreau became my friend, and Walden became an obsession of mine, while I bummed about the library and coffee shops by day. In the evenings, I'd cook dinner (which alternated between bangers and mash, and bubble and squeak) for my grandmother. Instead of doing something useful like, say, finding a job or signing on at the dole office, I retreated into a semi-rural subsistence-loving fantasy, all the while enjoying the creature comforts civilisation had to offer. Clearly it wasn't Thoreau's retreat into the wilderness that appealed to me most.

While I adored the simple pleasures he took in listening to birds sing, sowing beans in his meadow which sustained him all year, and his passion for civil disobedience and non-attachment to work and capitalism, I could never be like him. I was too gutless, too indecisive. The best I could do was pay a sort of homage to this new idol of mine. So, like Thoreau, I spent time in my local woods and wrote down everything I saw.

Spiritual enlightenment was a term I was wary of. I knew such a thing was probably a fantasy. But I did believe it was possible to feel contented with very little and that we humans have lost our intuition, ignoring the things that connect us to mother earth.

Wintry Wood was quite unlike Walden. For a start, no matter how deep you ventured into it, the drone of the M11 was inescapable. As were low-flying planes from nearby Stansted Airport. Sitting in the woods for extended periods was dull and uncomfortable at first. I couldn't grasp how ascetics and monks could retreat into such painfully dull surroundings. But then again, was I concentrating hard enough? I lacked the subtlety to grasp the natural pleasures. My mind wasn't pure like Thoreau's. It was too compromised. Instead of inner-serenity, the woods only made me more aware of myself, my ineptitude and failure as a human being. Instead of looking outwards, I peered inwards. Bremen occupied my thoughts, as did Nottingham and China. That feeling of oneness, of connectedness, of being able to appreciate annoying New Age platitudes, was absent. Completely absent. I returned home to Ninny with muddy shoes and a pissed-off look. So much for that failed transcendentalist escapade of mine.

Ninny provided a glimmer of hope: a light at the end of a tunnel of depression and the mental acrobatics I was doing every day. Negativity suffused every thought. I resented the world around me: every pedestrian, every cyclist, every waiter, every milkman. Exhaustion, presumably the result of an absence of motivation and purpose in my largely feckless existence, was dragging me back into a pool of leech-ridden despair. But Ninny chatted to me for hours about Hong Kong, about the elation of being with the others from the hostel, and about the subsequent melancholy I felt when we all went our separate ways. She got me. She'd experienced it all before. She was wise. The bitter pill that life was fragile, happiness was fleeting, and that it could all be hard to grasp didn't bother her. She remained quietly content with a schooner of sherry, her nice little Victorian cottage, her book on London during the war, and her evening prayers.

She's a simple Catholic lady. She never doubted the existence of a higher power, believing in an afterlife without the need to question the human condition or ponder the nature of reality. My existence on the other hand was all about doubt, constantly questioning things, finding faults in belief systems and ideologies and ever failing to resolve the infinite contradictions that presented themselves during discussions and intellectual arguments. I envied her simple faith, her childlike sincerity, and the way she prayed at her bedside every evening for all the family (and for her ailing friend Jeanette who was undergoing chemotherapy for leukaemia).

Her room, adorned with various Catholic paraphernalia, rosary beads and prayers by the various Saints, exuded warmth. I'd grown up in this tradition and the Catholic aesthetic in my home, but dismissed it all as mumbo jumbo. I'd never made the connection that perhaps her unwavering and earnest faith made her the nice person she was. The trouble was, the worst things in Catholicism were never too far from the front of mind. In fact the very word made me recoil. Believing or submitting to a higher power was hard enough, but all the attendant guilt and fear the religion engenders into its followers hardly seemed appealing to someone already riddled with guilt and fear. The sanctimony of many Christians put me off too, especially the childish game of religious one-upmanship played by the various denominations. It all seemed rather un-Christlike and rather pointless to me. I've never been overtly hostile to religion like one of those dickish New Atheists, but it's never grabbed me. I was sure in my mind that it was never really the vehicle towards becoming the self-actualised person I wanted to be.

Nonetheless, I still felt intrigued to know what made my grandmother tick. I started to read an old book she'd received on her nineteenth birthday from an old aunt. It was called *The Imitation of Christ*. It was ancient, battered and its wafer-thin pages had yellowed with age. At the same time, I'd borrowed a few selected readings from the Bhagavad Gita, which Thoreau alludes to periodically, and had started to skim-read Kerouac's *Dharma Bums*. In my mind—which craves logic, patterns and commonality in all things—I tried to reconcile my readings of ancient Eastern sages with that of Christ. Indeed one figure, Gautama Siddharta Buddha, stood out among the rest, both for his Christlike qualities and a world view suffused with sensitivity that made sense to me at that time. I read a few introductory teach-yourself Buddhism guides and visited a Buddhist centre in the East End. At the time it was a mere flirtation with a tradition which would subsequently have a greater effect on me than I could ever have imagined.

17. SEASON OF MISTS AND MELLOW FRUITFULNESS

IT WAS AUTUMN in England; in my opinion, the greatest of all the seasons. The weather was cool, the air was fresh and the trees shone a bright spectrum of red, orange and yellow. Life felt like a Keats poem. It was invigorating. During no other time in the year is one made quite as aware of the impermanence of physical phenomena and the natural dynamic cycle of birth and decay. The transient quality of the fall appealed to my pessimistic world view, which has always been tinged with melancholy. The Japanese have a term for it, *wabi sabi*, a philosophy which many Westerners struggle to grasp, but which is at the heart of traditional Japanese culture.

There was a lot of *wabi sabi* in Thoreau's sparsely furnished wood cabin, in his insistence on natural materials and his merging seamlessly with the natural environment of Walden Woods. Whereas art in the West has tended to favour perfection, precision and ornamentation, the Japanese Zen philosophers favoured a stripped-down aesthetic. Not a harsh bare minimalist one, but one devoid of the unnecessary. One that embraces the imperfect crooked quality of a handcrafted wooden spoon and the moss growing on the surface of stones. Finding *wabi sabi* in my little semi-rural English milieu became my hobby: whether in the moss-covered fading gravestones, the fallen leaves covering the cobbled streets, or the solitary birch tree in the high street. It provided a lens through which to see the world as tranquil. I took photos of things the easily-distracted work-obsessed denizen of the West would never think to find beauty in. The complexity of a bird's nest, the melancholy of a wilting leaf in a roadside kerb, the solemn beauty of a cracked terracotta vase. It touched me to appreciate the things that contained the essence of what it means to be part of this inevitable natural cycle. It made me feel calmer. It made me feel better.

That was until I got the call. The one I'd been dreading for a long time. My parents had found out about Nottingham. They knew now I had been a wretched morally-abject fraud who'd been deceiving them. Of course, they'd secretly known something was amiss the moment I absconded to China. But now they were tired of pussyfooting around me and probing, so my mum just asked me straight: did you get your degree or not? I came clean. Any more lies would've just been futile and, frankly, would've finished me off. It was a huge relief to me and my parents. After all this, they just wanted me to be straight with them. I admitted everything this time. That I just couldn't cope with university, the environment, the people, the workload, the noise, the parties. That I was struggling to function with life in general. They weren't angry. Even they realised university probably wasn't what it was cracked up to be. They didn't mind I hadn't acquired that bit of paper, along with the obligatory photo of me on the mantelpiece in a silly mortar board hat. They just wanted to see their son happy. I burst into floods of tears, telling my mum I just wanted to make her happy too.

I kept on trying. I had to keep on trying. As Keats summed up life in three words: *it goes on*. No amount of *wabi sabi*, Thoreau or ancient Hindu wisdom was going to save me. I needed a job. I needed a purpose. I needed a way to be independent.

18. CHINA REDUX

WITHOUT A DEGREE, I struggled to find gainful employment in a profession that had even a vague appeal. A vacancy at my local supermarket opened up, but I couldn't quite degrade myself that far. I guess I was work-shy. I hated the idea of wage slavery, of being the cog in a corporate juggernaut, of being in a position of subservience. At the same time I acknowledged the sort of people who do these jobs to be the true heroes of our time. The ones who endure painfully boring tasks, day in, day out for the promise of a wage that gives them few opportunities for self-advancement; or better yet, gives them the promise of a better life and education for their kids. I still can't imagine anything more heroic than that.

But I didn't have it in me at the time. I wasn't averse to work, but I did lack the self-esteem to function in a workplace and the amenability to sustain myself within it. With few options available, I began to entertain the possibility of again looking overseas for work. Spain seemed like a good place. Sun and sangria. Relaxed lifestyle. But no, I needed a degree to go there. There was Thailand with its pad thai, nice people and Buddhist temples. But no, a degree was necessary for there also. Ukraine maybe? Nope. I really didn't fancy the brutal socialist-realist architecture and steady diet of meat and potatoes (I hate potatoes)—I think it would have tipped me over the edge. Colombia? Forget it. I wasn't prepared to be kidnapped by left-wing militia groups living in the depths of the Amazon. China appeared to be the only option left. The only place where any unqualified cretin, as long as they're white, has the promise of a job. Whether it's posing in a suit and paid merely to turn up to functions to boost the company's face by having a European or American *associate*—I'm not joking by the way, a lot of Western expats pay their way in China by doing this—or working in some piece-of-shit teaching job, China is easy money. My mind was made up. China it was.

Ninny was going to miss me. We were good pals. She was way cooler than any of the people I'd known at school. She loved my company and the fact I'd sit patiently and listen to her for hours. She'd miss the cup of tea I'd bring up to her every morning, and I'd miss having someone to confide in, laugh and express deep feelings with.

But the thought of China still elicited an excitement in me. This time I could go there with a clean(er) conscience, unencumbered by the perpetual worry of my parents finding out the truth. This time I could go there and know what to expect. Instead of choosing a rural backwater, I did my research and found a reputable school in Beijing. At least there, there would be others like me with whom I could bitch about things and perhaps even strike up a friendship.

I began to think of the endless possibilities. Perhaps I'd share an evening like the one I'd had with that eclectic group of expats in Hong Kong, except we'd be drinking *baijiu* (a cheap, liver-eroding moonshine much beloved of the Chinese) and eating *jiaozi* (hearty meat-filled dumplings like ravioli) in a *hutong* (a traditional home that the government thought could be bulldozed during the Beijing Olympics, only to be met by a fierce and plucky local resistance). I imagined feeling on top of the world, sauntering around Tiananmen with a group of Canadians. Or perhaps I'd be lighting incense at a remote Buddhist monastery on the Mongolian steppe with some random Aussie backpackers. My mind raced through the permutations where this upcoming adventure could take me. I was so close to eating sweet, molasses-lacquered roast duck at Li Qun's, that I could already taste those delicious globules of fat.

After a long haul flight—which involved a painfully boring stopover in Russia staring at souvenirs emblazoned with the Russian flag, pictures of Putin (I wasn't quite aware how much of a personality-cult he was over there) and uniform rows of sweatshop-manufactured Russian dolls—I landed in Beijing, centre of the Chinese universe. It wasn't like the place I was in before in the South of China. People here were moneyed and spoke the standard Mandarin Chinese I'd learned from pop ballads and corny Chinese soap operas as a youngster. The city was huge. Really huge. A vast sprawl of dense-ly-packed high-rises enveloped by a thick smog. As my driver—a curly-haired northerner from Hebei called 'John' (I somehow doubt that was his real name)—drove me to my temporary digs, I could see myself living and functioning here. I had the language skills. I had an un-derstanding and appreciation of Chinese culture way be-yond that of the average Westerner. Hell, my chopstick skills alone were so on-point I was sure to make friends—perhaps not with fellow expats but at least with a bunch of Chinese.

After an hour stuck in the city's notorious traffic, we arrived in an unremarkable section of the city's eastern Haidian district. A gorgeous little white cat greeted me on my arrival. She belonged to the family next door, who I could hear from the chopping and stir-frying were busy preparing the family dinner. My flat, which was to be my home for two weeks of training, was modern and had all the amenities a Westerner required: internet, hot shower, a toilet that you actually sat on instead of squatted over and even, luxury of all luxuries, a soft mattress. I shared this cosy little space with a guy called David, a scrawny military brat from DC. He was unfazed by China. He'd lived in practically every corner of the globe and was unmoved by my enthusiasm and the effeminate way I waxed poetical about the East. We were polar opposites but, over a bottle of Tsingtao later that evening, we got on okay.

After waking up at 4am the next day, unable to sleep and heavy around the eyes with jet lag, I ventured out into the city. David was still concussed. He'd had a much longer plane journey than me which had involved a stay in Amsterdam and Frankfurt. Restless, I ventured out into this vast urban jungle hoping to have a few epiphanies along the way. After a hearty breakfast of pork buns and hot soy milk from a local street stand frequented by construction workers (the rate of construction in Beijing is phenomenal and cranes are a regular feature of its skyline), I headed by subway for Tiananmen. It seemed the logical place to begin my second China odyssey.

Even at 5am the square was packed. The atmosphere there was tense and oppressive, as inscrutable security guards in reflective sunglasses monitored your every move. To get a sense of the scale of its vast space, you have to experience it in person. It's so big it wears you out just walking from one end to the other. Being there, at the centre of the Chinese universe, made me feel as though I'd ascended Everest. I'd finally made it to the summit and this was only the beginning.

Later that day, after running around the city's rabbit

warren of old *hutongs* in a supercharged and frenzied state, devouring every available morsel of street food and soaking up every drop of culture, I totally crashed. Jet lag had crept up on me and I was hit by a wall of fatigue. But I kept on going and eventually got a second wind.

That evening, I was invited for dinner by a colleague at the school. He was a maniacal foodie like me, so we had some common ground at first. When David arrived a little bit later, I struggled to talk. The two of us talking was fine, but the gruff American's presence altered the dynamic and I felt completely at sea. Instead of going out drinking in Sanlitun, I made my excuses and headed home to Haidian. Besides, training the next day began at 8am and I needed the rest.

The next day, the omens were good. The sun was bright, the sky was blue and for once there was no pollution. I excelled in every aspect of training. My experience teaching in Chinese Hicksville had prepared me well. The kids in Beijing were a doddle in comparison to those naughty Southerners in Fujian and were scarily bright and quick to learn. This was the real deal compared to the last place. Of all the fellow trainees, I scored the highest marks on assessment day. I was pretty chuffed with myself seeing as nobody I knew back home had me down as a teacher. I'd grasped the technique and was 'acing it', as they say.

That night I celebrated, thankfully not with the fellow Brits and Americans I was training with but with a few Chinese businessmen at the company. I felt safer around them, less exposed for my social inadequacies: they wouldn't be able to tell if I said something inappropriate and if they did they'd simply put it down to me being a bumbling unsophisticated Westerner. The dinner was a glorious feast consisting of typical Dongbei cuisine: lots of sweet belly pork in delicious sauces, an array of seasoned vegetables and an obligatory main of the most succulent Peking duck I'd ever eaten. Snowflake beer and Chinese spirits were drunk in unholy quantities throughout the meal. I was so full I had to waddle home afterwards.

19. DINNER FOR THREE

AFTER THE TEN DAYS training were up in Beijing, I was assigned to a school in a city a few hundred miles south (spitting distance in Chinese terms) called Zhengzhou, a rapidly expanding megalopolis of 10 million people and counting. The train journey was four-and-a-half-hours of flat, intensively-farmed arable farmland and 400 miles of solid smog. A guy next to me crunched his way through a big bag of sunflower seeds throughout the entire journey. I wanted to punch his lights out. My head was pounding after a couple of shots of *Moutai* (a really potent Chinese liqueur) I'd been forced to down at the leaving dinner the night before, and my poor abused stomach and liver had both gone on strike. I really wasn't in the mood for the train journey, or the thought of being greeted by representatives of some poor Chinese school out in the sticks that were pinning all their hopes on some slovenly, unshaven Western pig who was still hungover from the night before.

After the excruciating train ride, I disembarked at Zhengzhou and waited next to a Burger King at the front entrance. Nobody was there to greet me. Had they forgotten? Or were they just late? Turns out they were waiting for me at the wrong station at the other end of the city.

I had time at least to stop and observe my surroundings. Compared to Beijing, this place felt a little backward. I was the only white face in town once again. Outside the main station, which was an ant colony of activity, country folk from the surrounding villages, towns and provinces hauled all their earthly possessions in Ikea holdalls and carrier bags. Men with rotten teeth smoked cheap, tar-laden Chinese cigarettes, while women fed babies rice and vegetables with wooden chopsticks. I could gaze at these people for hours. They were endlessly fascinating to me.

Before long two guys from the school arrived to collect me. Even by Asian standards these two guys seemed feminine; both were painfully skinny, wore tight-fitting pastel-coloured clothes from Uniqlo and spoke in high-pitched voices. I could tell they were gay, and sure enough they were, even if they would never dare admit it (in China, being gay still isn't acceptable). One was called Jeven (he told me it was from some American sitcom) and the other Cooper (after his favourite car, the Mini).

Typical of Chinese face-giving, they took me out that evening to eat in an expensive restaurant. I didn't want to eat and I could barely even muster light conversation with these guys. After the *Moutai* and the four hour train ride with my nerves on edge from the seed-munching jackass next to me, I just wanted to crash out and forget the world outside even existed. But no. I had to eat. I had to drink. And I had to be the charming inoffensive guest. I really couldn't be arsed, but soldiered on and carried out my duty. The BBQ fish we ate was picked by Jeven from a fish tank, bonked over the head and cooked up in a dish of vegetable and chilli broth. To be honest, it was delicious. It revived me and cured my hangover. I went to bed that night in yet another new apartment feeling satiated and comfortable. Tomorrow I was to meet my new colleague, Jade.

20. MY WORKMATE, THE DRUGGIE

I WAS ONE OF TWO foreign teachers at the school. My co-worker was an Australian girl called Jade. She wasn't exactly what I'd expected. She was all over the place: a scatterbrain, a hothead, a dreamer, a poet, an artist, an ex-meth junkie—a train wreck of an individual. Her speech was mumbled and incomprehensible, her mannerisms and movements being erratic and quite disturbing at times. And then there was her apartment. It made my hovel in Bremen look like a *ryokan* in rural Japan. It was dirty, damp, mouldy, greasy, stinky and covered in unwashed clothes. It wasn't fit for human habitation. I couldn't quite believe someone could live like this. But Jade didn't seem to care. She didn't shave her armpits. She barely ever showered, only doing so when her BO offended the sleazy, low-life Chinese playboys with a white-girl fetish who would often approach her in the street.

However, once you looked past her slightly scary, mad-haired appearance, she wasn't that bad. Realising she was to be my colleague for the next year or so, I thought it best to be on good terms with her. So after dinner at a Korean BBQ place on the second night, we went for a beer at the local bar. It became our regular haunt after work. And it was a great place to sit, eat copious piles of complimentary melon seeds (which are really tasty by the way and perfect beer food) and drink very overpriced imported lagers from Korea, Germany and Australia. The theme was Maoist kitsch and the bar was littered with relics from the communist era. We had a great time there and, being the few white faces, attracted a lot of attention—not all of it good.

One evening, an especially obnoxious nouveau-riche type invited us to the karaoke bar he owned. As he staggered blind-drunk towards our table, he even managed to spill his beer all over my lap. Yet stupidly Jade still agreed to get in his Mercedes and be driven by him to the venue. Assuming the role of her protective father, I went with them. I didn't want him or his gang of rich-pig-friends to rape her. It was terrifying. My heart was in my mouth the whole way there. He drove like a madman and almost crashed into a lamppost. When we arrived, his multi-story KTV (a karaoke complex with lots of separate karaoke rooms for hire), was empty.

Immediately, I felt panic. The earth moved beneath my feet. I felt another attack coming along. It had been a while and one was long overdue. My thoughts were racing and I'd convinced myself this guy—the most loathsome pig of a man with no manners, fake jewellery, chains and a Tag Heuer watch—had lured us into his private club only to drug us and harvest our precious organs (this has happened to unsuspecting foreigners in China before). We would wake up the next morning with crude stitching on our abdomen on a grubby surgeon's table, staring at our kidneys in jars on the table next to us. I grabbed Jade by the arm, who by now barely knew where she was, and told her we had to go. She of course refused. Fuck. We were going to die. I readied myself.

But no. It was worse than death. It was, after such catastrophic thoughts of being butchered and discarded by black market organ harvesters, just plain old karaoke. With a bunch of really boring guys. And I do mean really boring. I hated karaoke. I cowered away whenever somebody passed me the microphone and begged me to sing something by Wang Lee Hom or Jay Chou. It was my worst nightmare and it was something all Chinese, especially my work colleagues, liked to do way too often.

21. THE HAT INCIDENT

THE TEACHING here was easier, but still a bit stressful. It got more so after Jade, rather predictably, jacked it all in and ran back to Melbourne. She'd become jittery and irascible from several months of drug withdrawal. Every conversation we had together in the 'Chairman Mao Bar', as we affectionately called our old faithful, invariably became her launching into a one-sided, half-drunk tirade against China's draconian drug laws and that somehow legalising all drugs would eliminate people's need to take them. She made no coherent sense any more. She was pining for meth-induced highs, cracked-out delirium or at least a big toke of Humboldt County's finest. In China she couldn't get them—at least not without considerable risk of arrest, imprisonment, interrogation, deportation or, worse still, being strapped to a chair and injected with lethal amounts of toxins. I told her in no uncertain terms to leave her drug habits at home or, failing that, to get the hell out of China. And she did. She pulled a famous midnight run. The school paid me double in her absence, which I couldn't complain about.

Not being able to tolerate trips to karaoke with my Chinese co-workers every other night, I went to the bar on my own. It was there I met some of the few foreigners who, like me, felt a bit like Bill Murray's culturally-alienated character in *Lost in Translation*. The first guy was a big red-haired Finn living in the Hilton across the street. The second was a feckless, super-chilled-out South African guitar teacher. The third was a rebellious Indian medical student. We became an unlikely clique who were all odd and dysfunctional in our own ways. I was subsumed into this motley assortment of characters, each with slightly chequered pasts (every foreigner in China it seemed was running away from something back home). Though we stuck together and occasionally ventured out of the bar together, I never genuinely felt entirely comfortable with them. I felt lost in the group, unable to go with the flow.

The guys did things I didn't want to join in with, but nonetheless felt obliged to. Their favourite thing to do was to down unholy quantities of a truly vile and hideous mixture of whisky and ice tea—this was a popular way to disguise the taste of a drink that is fashionable in China but unpalatable to most young Chinese—whilst hanging out in the gaudiest Western-style nightclubs mainly frequented by a bunch of nouveau riche poseurs bankrolled by their rich daddies. These guys shamelessly abused their foreign privilege, waltzed into the nightclubs without paying, and boasted about the properties they owned back home in a bid to lure unsuspecting Asian women to bed. I hated it. I hated the nightclubs we went to, especially the one particularly pretentious place we seemed to frequent called Muse.

The place was a faux-Greco-Roman hellhole with fake columns, frescos and private booths upholstered with pink velour. It was crammed full of bored-looking Asian gumars glued to their smartphones while their chauvinistic boyfriends smoked and drank counterfeit bottles of Remy Martin to impress their cohort of equally empty-headed companions. I felt conspicuously unfashionable in there—I wasn't a poseur by any stretch. I felt appalled and vaguely intimidated by the level of narcissism on display, so much so that I decided to cover my rapidly thinning thatch with a baseball cap before entering.

The fourth time we went there, my cap—which was discoloured by salty sweat marks from wearing it too much—was promptly ripped off by some obnoxious lout in the club. The whole club laughed and I felt in that very moment like dying. The only person who felt my pain was the Indian medical student, Aryan or AJ as he was known in his alma mater of Denver University in Colorado. He promptly put the cap back on my head, backwards, and dragged me out of the Babylon that was Muse Nightclub. (The nightclub has since been closed down due to drug activity. The fate of those drug dealers, many of whom were Africans who hung around the toilets, remains a mystery. It haunts me to think of their fate which, in totalitarian China, was most likely the death penalty).

Another evening, one that has left an indelible mark in my mind, the guys lead me down an uninviting-looking alley. I asked them where we were headed. The Finn replied: *Somewhere good. You'll like it.* Turns out it was brothel, a decrepit hovel in some crumbling, derelict apartment block in an especially slummy part of a generally slummy city. I imagined such places existed only in the Victorian East End. I felt panic. How the hell was I going to get out of this one? I tried to make my excuses, but the big Finn wasn't having any of it and dragged me into a dimly-lit, grimy little room with a torn purple futon.

A few sour-faced, bored-looking, gum-chewing Chinese whores in cheap high heels were on their smartphones. The Finn was intent for us all to prove our manliness, likely suspecting that I—by far the least-alpha-male of the bunch—wasn't up to the job. Indeed, I've never had sex before. In fact, the very idea of it repulses me—I am definitely not in tune with my base instincts. He commanded me to choose one. So I picked the least attractive, a round-faced older lady with smooth legs. I had no intention of doing anything anyway.

In a musty-smelling pink-walled room riddled with damp, with a tiny sink, a waste paper basket full of tissues and condoms and a hard stained mattress, the dispassionate whore pulled down my pants. I pushed her away and said I didn't want to do anything with her. She resisted, and so did I. Eventually, I took an extra 100 Yuan out of my pocket, thrust it at the bemused girl, pulled up my pants and stormed out. I wasn't having any more.

I never contacted the guys again, except for AJ. I still had a soft spot for him and was still grateful to him for rescuing me from the derision of mocking revellers in that awful nightclub. We shared a few meals together. I cooked him a spaghetti with anchovies and capers at mine. They were basically all the Western ingredients I could cobble together in the supermarket's overpriced imported section. To return the favour, he cooked me a chicken curry in his crummy student digs using a rudimentary selection of utensils. It still tasted bloody good. It had been a while since I'd had decent Indian food, and I savoured every bite of it.

22. BUDGET SURGERY

A J, A PRIVILEGED well-spoken Brahmin from a very wealthy family back home in Hyderabad, loved being away from his strict family back home in India. It meant he could party without being castigated by his strict Indian father, and was able to get away with eating 'non-veg' (his particular caste being strict vegetarians who even went as far as not eating certain root vegetables). Though a thoroughly inconsistent Hindu, AJ had a real heart of gold and would do everything he could to help people. So much so he even had a solution to the intractable problem of my premature baldness; one he claimed would make me 'the perfect man'.

Being a medical student in one of Henan Province's biggest hospitals, he had connections with—who he claimed to be—the best doctors and surgeons in China. Using the best of these connections, he got me in the next day to have a consultation with Mrs Lee, allegedly one of China's best plastic surgeons who was pioneering a new method of hair transplant called FUE (Follicular Unit Extraction). It involved a long painstaking harvesting of hair follicles from the back to the front of the head, beginning at nine in the morning and finishing at nine in the evening. AJ and I negotiated a cut-price deal: the full surgery would cost just 20,000 RMB or roughly 2,000 pounds—so long as I paid Mrs Lee in cash and agreed to have the surgery done in her 'private headquarters' (a back-street apartment that she'd rented to do cut-price surgeries outside of the hospital). It was all highly dodgy in retrospect, but this was China. Anything goes there and provided you have the money to pay for it, you can get any sort of surgery you like.

AJ and I met Mrs Lee in the centre of the city outside the Erqi memorial in central Zhengzhou. She was in sunglasses and a long coat. It almost felt like an episode of *Candid Camera* or *Trigger Happy TV*. We were guided to a nearby block of flats and the grottiest room I'd ever seen. This really was backstreet surgery. My heart sank. I handed her the thick wad of cash I'd bunged into my rucksack and took the plunge. The surgery was painful in places. I had to suppress panic attacks throughout as I lay prostrate the entire time. But I made it through. And, despite the initial apprehension, it actually turned out pretty well.

On the way back, I had to wear a bag over my head to protect the newly inserted follicles. In the rickshaw back to AJ's apartment, my head started bleeding. Luckily AJ was on hand with a packet of wet wipes. He'd waited the entire 12 hours outside. He had a real heart of gold that guy. When we got back to his, he insisted I took his bed. He propped up my head with a couple of pillows, to ensure the newly inserted hair follicles didn't fall out, and cooked me a South Asian egg curry that set my mouth on fire. Thankfully he had mango lassi and lashings of cardamom tea on hand to put it out. What a nice guy. I was touched by his unconditional kindness. He did it purely to relieve my anxiety, to help me out. I slept well that night feeling cared for and loved.

In the morning, we were both eager to see the results. It looked good. My bald patch at the front was no longer visible. A couple of months of growth and it would appear seamless with the rest of my otherwise thick thatch. We were both amazed by what a success it had been. I looked good. I felt good. I had a new-found confidence. AJ said to me: *Now go find your girl, bro. The right one will love you exactly how you are.* And that's what I did. I went out and found my girl. She was to be my introduction to the bittersweet reality of romance and relationships.

23. A SHORT-LIVED ROMANCE WITH WENDY WEI

I ONLY REALLY HAD TO TAKE MY PICK of girls. Being a white foreigner I had sufficient cultural capital, despite not being especially good-looking, to still be considered a prize catch. But I knew I ought to choose wisely. Chinese girls, though on the surface seem light ethereal creatures, have a reputation for being dragon ladies underneath—with hot tempers and an alarming tendency to fly unexpectedly off the handle, throw paddies in busy public places and root through your mobile phone to check you aren't cheating on them.

So, I picked Wendy. She certainly wasn't the prettiest, or the most outgoing. In fact, by Chinese standards, she was plain and perhaps even a little bit ugly. It wasn't her looks so much that attracted me to her. It was her simplicity and plainness; her quiet unassuming nature appealed to me more than the meretricious beauty of many other girls with beanpole physiques, caked in white make-up and wearing freaky contact lenses that made their eyes look bigger. There was no vicious streak, no insidious narcissism and, as far as I could tell, no tendency to act like a spoilt brat if she wasn't receiving all the attention she craved.

I also felt sorry for her. She was 29 and unmarried which, while nothing out of the ordinary in the West, is considered just a stone's throw from being a so-called *leftover* in China. And marriage in a highly-conformist collectivist society like China is considered life's ultimate purpose. Personal dreams, ambitions, aspirations and travel plans are superfluous Western ideas contrary to Confucian-Marxist ideals. We should be grateful in the West we aren't bound by such stifling outdated conventions where, despite all the surface modernity and the rush to emulate capitalist America, the Chinese mentality remains deplorably old-fashioned and many of the people are near-feudal in their outlook.

After a couple of dates at a coffee shop, I asked her out. She said I'd made her the happiest girl in China. I must say, I felt a little perturbed by this. I knew, in my heart of hearts, I wasn't going to be able to maintain this. I was too prone to push the self-destruct button. I wasn't going to be able to socialise with her friends. What if she railroaded me into a marriage proposal? A million disturbing thoughts flooded into my mind at once.

We had a relaxing time at first. She was a local (or *Zhengzhou-ren*) and she knew the city's labyrinthine streets inside out. She introduced me to peculiar delicacies I'd never eaten (which included deep-fried soy cockroaches and tempura-battered flower blossom no less). She was my go-to guide for all things Chinese. She introduced me to her wonderfully hospitable family who, despite living together in a cramped apartment and looking after their elderly relatives with hunchbacks and bendy legs, prepared a banquet of some of the best Chinese food I'd ever eaten. Truly wonderful. I even made pals with her adorable 4-year-old niece who'd adopted the charmingly innocent English name 'Rainbow'. After lunches of stir-fried veggies, red-braised pork, lamb noodles, and tomato and egg soup, I'd sit with Rainbow on the sofa, reading to her in English. It felt normal, as though finally I was doing something that regular people did.

Things got a little tricky however when I invited her to my apartment. I felt uneasy around physical contact, even hugging was unnatural to me. She craved intimacy and, being my wrought-up self, I was unable to give it. Frustration was etched on her face, which became sourer the longer we sat on my futon, a few inches apart, unable to make conversation. I didn't know what to say other than to offer her some dragon fruit and yoghurt, the only two foods I had in my fridge. She grabbed her coat and took a cab home. A few hours later, she texted me explaining how embarrassed she felt. I guess my socially-inept autistic brain has its limits, especially when unravelling the mysteries of relationships and physical and emotional intimacy between two human beings. I'd tried my best to fake my way through it; I had even recited lines from romance films. But when it came to sex, I was all at sea. It embarrassed me. The idea of taking my clothes off and having to touch somebody, allowing them to breathe and sweat on me, was frankly horrifying. I know she wanted this, and I felt guilty for neglecting her because of my own failings as a male specimen. The whole incident was a hammer-blow to my self-esteem and my sense of place in the world. It sent me back into a cocoon of nihilistic cynicism.

After that, I stopped caring about her. I gave up on things, including showering. It was Bremen and Nottingham all over again, except this time there was a clear and definite trigger. This was all linked to my outsiderism. I have a thin skin and my self-esteem had plummeted after my awkward sexual encounter with Wendy. I felt as though it undermined my whole existence, my fragile identity as a male. So, yet again, I sunk into the black hole of depression.

24. NADIR

MY APARTMENT on the 23rd floor had become a cesspit of broken sesame crackers, green tea bottles and festering, half-eaten, instant noodle containers. Clothes lay scattered on the floor. I'd stopped responding to Wendy's phone calls and messages on WeChat (the Chinese state-sanctioned version of WhatsApp). She'd become ultra-clingy, and going a single day without calling her or sending her some saccharine heart-shaped emoticon on WeChat meant I could expect a barrage of phone calls and messages. It started to piss me off big time and I really started to resent her. Get lost. Leave me the fuck alone. I can't be a proper loving boyfriend to you. Stop calling me.

I got so lazy I didn't get up until 20 minutes before my first class. Instead of a 10p bus ride, I'd take expensive cab rides to work. I didn't care. I didn't bother shaving and before long began to look like a real hobo. Despite my steady diet of junk food—which consisted of a tube of fake Chinese Pringles, a packet of Oreos and a bottle of ice tea for dinner—I lost weight and became whip-thin. My mind and body were both disintegrating rapidly.

Wendy eventually lost interest in me. I'd been the worst sort of boyfriend: aloof, uncaring, selfish, neglectful and unable to show affection, averse even to holding hands and hugging. She clung to a vague hope of marriage which, in my deplorable state, was utterly ridiculous. Some people my age were starting families; I on the other hand struggled to wear matching socks every day. At the same time, my job as a teacher sucked big time. The cloying cuteness of the Chinese kids, the faking it as a teacher, the whole grovelling to a bunch of coarse pot-bellied fathers in Nike tracksuits with bottomless funds just wore thin. Breathing in air comparable to sucking on a car exhaust was making me feel permanently rundown. After surviving over a year in this place, I decided to call it quits. Without telling a soul, I threw my life back into a suitcase and made a beeline for Beijing.

The train journey was incredibly wrenching. Although I hated my rut, I was also loath to leave it. It was one of the most confusing times of my life. I couldn't decide what it really was in life I wanted. Once in Beijing, I even considered turning back: to start afresh and clean up my act again in Zhengzhou. But that ship had sailed. If I had wanted to get it together, I would have done so already. It was too late. I had to forget the life I had started to build in Zhengzhou and somehow managed to squander. I needed to go back to the UK and get help.

At about midnight, I checked into an Ibis hotel near

to the airport. It was a weird spot. People actually lived ordinary Chinese lives here not far from the runway, cooking garlic and pak choi in woks out in the open. I don't think I ever felt more alone and more detached from humanity than I did here. Two Russian businessmen drank at the bar, while I smoked an entire packet of one pound *hongqiqu* which are quite possibly the nastiest lowest-grade cigarettes on the planet. They made me throw up in my room later. I went to bed with the taste of an ashtray and vomit in my mouth.

The next day I didn't quite feel as bad. In fact I was relishing returning to a place where I could once again breathe fresh air, eat cheese, drink coffee and, most importantly, remain anonymous. Like my previous exit out of China, I paid in cash with a wad of Yuan I'd withdrawn out of my bank account. The rest of the wages I'd saved during the year were now wedged between my boxer shorts in my suitcase. At the airport with bags of time to spare, I said one final goodbye to Wendy by phone. She was sad to see me go and wished me the very best. I guess it had dawned on her I had problems. She wasn't bitter or resentful about me going. I was sad to leave her though. She had never been bad towards me.

London seemed like toytown compared to Zhengzhou. Embarrassingly low-rise and small compared to the vast Asian megalopolis I'd stayed in. The journey from Heathrow to Epping seemed to pass by in minutes.

I was a seasoned traveller now, but being home felt like the biggest culture shock of them all.

25. BIBLIOTHERAPY

NOW BACK HOME in the UK, I vowed to get myself better. I'd distrusted psychiatry before but was prepared to give it another go. It was an agonising 12-week wait to see a psychiatrist. In the meantime, I was still deteriorating and barely managed to make it out of bed in the mornings. Worse still, I'd started to show signs of Obsessive Compulsive Disorder. In my case the theme of language, something of a special interest, had now turned into a full-blown obsession from which I couldn't escape. In fact, analysing it occupied pretty much every waking hour and it only worsened my depression and anxiety.

Indeed, the psychiatrist I eventually got to see diagnosed a complex constellation of disorders based on the symptoms and behaviours I'd described: anhedonia (lack of pleasure in doing things), anxiety, panic disorder, severe depression, OCD, BDD, OPD, autism. The list went on. It destroyed my self-esteem to have so many labels pinned to me like that. And the treatments they were offering like CBT (Cognitive Behavioural Therapy) seemed about as useful to me as a chocolate fireguard.

The follow-up psychologist I saw made me lose my faith in psychiatry altogether. She hadn't even bothered reading my notes prior to the session. She was so vague, limp and insipid, I began to wonder why I'd bothered coming home.

I had to find a solution. A sympathetic GP suggested *bibliotherapy* and gave me an extensive list of prescribed literature. Some were about CBT, some gave a bit more generic advice on how to eat and live, and an awful lot of books seemed to be about *mindfulness*—the media's new favourite buzzword synonymous with mental well-being and equanimity. Mindfulness is at the very heart of Buddhist psychology. It isn't so much a New Age fad as an ancient practice designed to achieve a liberation from the bombardment of negative thoughts which stem from our 'monkey minds'.

I sought refuge in such an attitude, one of focussing on the present. But, being me, I wanted to go beyond the prescribed reading list and delve deeper into the heart of Eastern wisdom. In essence, I went back to the Buddhism I'd touched on during my brief dalliance with *wabi sabi*. My first reference point was the Buddhism of Tibet, or Mahayana Buddhism to be more precise. It's emphasis on mindful compassion and altruism seemed impressively reasonable. Books by the great spiritual masters of Tibet and Bhutan articulated their ideas in a way that is understandable to the Western mind. The benign simplicity of Matthieu Ricard, a long-time meditator reputed to be the happiest man alive according to neuroscience, had a particular impact on me. It's not often that somebody writes in such a way that is so totally sincere it moves you, but his book *Happiness* is one I'd recommend to anyone, especially those afflicted by mental illness. The loving-kindness he extols is the perfect antidote to afflictive emotions like depression and anxiety—shifting excessive inward-looking attention outward to others who may also be suffering.

After practising the type of meditation he prescribes in the book, I quickly began to feel its effects. Focussing for 15 minutes a day on positive altruistic feelings towards others really was reinforcing positivity in my daily behaviour. I began organising my routine around others, buying spontaneous gifts for my family, donating to charity and just generally being nicer. People remarked on how cheerful I seemed, how kind I was and how helpful I was being. I wasn't used to hearing these sorts of remarks in reference to me. This Buddhist stuff wasn't mumbo jumbo after all; it was actually working.

26. DESIRING NOT TO DESIRE

BUDDHISM'S CENTRAL PREMISE is the acceptance that life is suffering. Eliminating the toxins of anger, jealousy and fear completely is a difficult process for anyone, let alone a person with autistic traits, but according to Buddhist psychology it is essential for achieving a balanced mind free from this suffering. This practice goes way beyond meditation and requires you to adopt kinder gentler habits in every aspect of your daily life. Meditation is a way of cultivating positive emotions, but in and of itself is useless. Unless you strive to carry on what you discover through meditation, there is very little point to it.

So, every day I did this. Instead of being the cynical little git I am accustomed to being, I began to delight in the fact others were happy instead of constantly envying and criticising them. I began to smile more and allow anger and frustration to pass—refusing to fan their flames—until, inevitably, they would die down again. Like many autists, I am particularly bothered by loud noises and sensory overload (it's said we experience sound more intensely than *neurotypicals*). I had to find a way to counter my reptilian instinct to react aversely to them. I had to realise that anger was a symptom of fear, and that fear—other than when it forces you to react to imminent danger—has no rational basis.

Buddhist psychology encourages you to stop and work through emotions like anger, to calmly put things into their correct perspective. One of the tenets of the Eightfold Path is *Right Thought* and, as an OCD sufferer, I found this to be especially relevant. My obsessive compulsive tendencies had led to unhealthy fixations and unrealistic outlooks on reality. I finally had to rationalise that these fixations, though a symptom of my condition, were causing me to suffer. So, I vowed to break free from rigid patterns of thinking for good by recognising them and slowly sending them in different directions.

27. CONTEMPLATING ONE'S NAVEL

BUDDHISM IS, in a sense, more psychology than religion. It doesn't have a doctrine. It doesn't have a creed. The concept of *dharma* isn't an inviolable law so much as a method. It's a discussion and a dialectic that encourages scepticism and probes the nature of things. It lends itself to a conquest of the mind more so than religion. Dharma isn't ordained by superiors like vicars or priests, and Buddhism itself has no formal clergy. The religion is essentially non-theistic; it doesn't concern itself with the Abrahamic concept of a stern, capricious and omnipresent grandfather figure watching over his little creations.

Worrying about whether or not 'God' exists is facile and one bound to end in pointless cyclical debates. Such a question is not going to free your mind. This was the sort of enlightenment that made sense to me just as the spiritual, yet secular-minded, Thoreau did a couple of years back—when encumbered by a need to impress others or to conform, he set out by himself to Walden

Woods in a bid to discover truth. Previously I'd never been able to throw in with a particular ideology or religion, but with Buddhism I found a way to preserve my individuality whilst finding freedom from being myself. Indeed, it was a way to retain the strengths my autistic traits conferred—like excellent concentration on one particular subject—and use it to cultivate positive mindframes instead of the negative ones that were threatening to destroy me.

Like Thoreau, who retreated into the woods to discover the essence of life, Buddhists endeavour to find who they are by going it alone, without the imposition of a higher power and without having others ascribing roles to them. It necessitates going into yourself and listening to silence in order to escape the rat race of existence—the cycle of birth and death—the *samsara*. The illusion that something is there, that a magical, instant, quick-fix outward solution exists to your internal chaos causes many to suffer. As the estimable Eastern philosopher Alan Watts puts it: *You're forever the donkey with a carrot suspended in front of it.* A Buddha is someone who has awakened from *samsara*. Someone who is free from illusion. Someone who is balanced and moderate.

What I needed was something like *The Middle Way*—one that didn't necessitate throwing on an orange robe, shaving my head and absconding to a remote Himalayan mountaintop just to spend three decades contemplating the shape and dimensions of a pine cone. That isn't Buddhism, or at least not a variety that I wanted or would advise anyone to follow. What I needed was a path that gave me a practical way to cope with suffering and the personal dissatisfaction I felt in my life. Becoming a monk definitely wasn't the answer. Besides, I wasn't going to renounce myself, my twice-daily espresso, my laptop and my beloved YouTube. I wasn't going to deny my Western roots or my Western conditioning either. A superficial attraction to the exotic patina of Eastern mystical tradition is something the estimable Dalai Lama himself warns his Western followers against. Asceticism made as little sense to me as did mindless self-indulgence and pleasure-seeking: both are forms of suffering. A radical solution was not what I needed.

Balance is what I required most, and the Buddhist path is one of perfect balance and moderation. It gives up the quest of taking the world by storm. It gives up finding an answer to life's unsolvable questions and unravelling the mystery of our universe. There is no holier-than-thou attitude like in Christianity. Calling yourself a Buddhist is in and of itself vain and problematic. Conceptualisation, labelling and ascribing words to a thing is what schools like Zen warn against. The Zen tradition, which I began reading about, is appealing to many Westerners seeking a more enlightened lifestyle, though I'd imagine very few grasp its essential meaning. I for one found it so cryptic, so confusing and so counter-intuitive that I gave up reading about it.

As per the Dalai Lama's advice, I consulted a faith that was more culturally appropriate to me. The one I had some connection to, but knew little about. On a cold Friday morning, I headed up to the top of the hill where the church was. I felt a little bit strange; places like this had a knack of putting a secular type like me on edge and certainly wasn't a place I'd ever imagined stepping into in a time of crisis. I also felt a bit of a hypocrite; I hadn't set foot in one of these for the better part of a decade.

28. A LITTLE CATHOLIC MEDITATION

I **WAS BAPTISED** a Catholic. My forefathers were all devout, but I was raised in a non-observant household very much outside the faith. The closest I got to it was my grandmother getting me to recite Our Father every time I visited her as child. I never warmed to religion, especially one as dogmatic and guilt-ridden as Catholicism, preferring instead to doubt and question things. Still, the aesthetic held a certain appeal. I liked the ornate frescoes, the intricate designs and I especially loved the smell of incense in the churches. So I felt at home in the local Catholic church, even if it was just to get a bit of peace and quiet. I had grown up with this style, with wooden crosses, Jesus figurines and Virgin Mary candle-holders in the house—more for decoration than for their symbolism. It made sense me being here. Not being religious doesn't necessarily make me any less Catholic, I think.

One day I entered the church with a new-found openness to the spiritual benefits of religion after my dilettantish foray into Buddhism. It was there that, to my surprise,

I spotted an advert for a meditation group held once a week at the church. You wouldn't immediately think that a conservative tradition like Catholicism would be open to the idea of combining Eastern contemplative practices with Bible study and seeking unity with Christ. I was intrigued by the mixing of influences and went along.

A small group, largely composed of Christians with a slightly Gnostic, mystical bent (or at least a vague penchant for New Age practices promoted by the likes of Oprah Winfrey) would sit in contemplative silence each Friday morning in the Our Lady Chapel, in much the same way Buddhists describe, to cultivate feelings of empathy, well-being and compassion. It was great to see two distinct cultures thinking alike. I joined a few of these and enjoyed, more than anything, discussing my ideas with the lady who was organising the sessions. Her mystical understanding of Catholicism chimed with the Eastern Buddhist ideas I had been reading about and she was very open to blending the two. I liked her a lot.

Moreover, I was starting to come out of my shell a bit more. The Buddhist tenet of *Right Speech* made me consider the feelings of others more when I spoke to them and, for the first time, I wasn't boring people silly: I slowed down a bit and gave people a chance to speak. And it was paying dividends. People, more-to-the point my follow countrymen in my native England, were genuinely happy to talk to me for a change.

After the meditation, I'd go out with two ladies: one a chatterbox, the other a mother of four, known among her friends as the best curry chef in town. One day, I invited them both for coffee at the Madeiran café. For the first time, I wasn't going in there alone. I had the company of others and not just a strong coffee and a newspaper to amuse me. I felt relaxed, not permanently on edge worrying about what the other person may or may not have been thinking and second-guessing everything. I was totally at ease and could've spent hours talking about banal topics I had no real interest in. The conversation topic was irrelevant, it was the friendship we all showed towards one other that meant everything. The two ladies did indeed become my good friends. We had a beautiful platonic thing going on which never felt strained or awkward. It felt natural, and natural is something I'd rarely been acquainted with until now. Natural to an autistic person can, paradoxically, feel totally unnatural. For once though, this wasn't the case.

29. THE REAL ME IS NOT ME

IN THE EAST, people are part of a collective. The Chinese don't generally like to stand out. They favour modesty instead of outward displays of egocentricity. In the West, we are the opposite: we are encouraged to be individualistic. We strive to do anything to protect our separate selves. In that sense we are extremely naïve because, ultimately, there exists no self. We are but an extension of the world. The extreme naivety of egocentrism is especially pronounced in people like me with traits of autism. Autism itself stems from the Greek *autos* meaning 'self', and our sense of self is far greater than the average human being. That doesn't mean we necessarily want to stand out, but very often we do because of our inherent separateness, through our failure to show empathy and physical and emotionally intimacy.

Buddhism's ethos is about trying not to desire and therefore not to feed this illusion of self. During my years, I had been stuck in a cycle of isolation and of desire. I'd wanted things I couldn't have. But now, I had a means to break free from this habit. The key to liberation was within me and the first step was to accept who I was. I learned to accept my idiosyncrasies. The ones that lead me to suffer in the past no longer bothered me. It no longer mattered to me if others thought I was a bit odd. Ultimately thoughts are irrelevant and illusory in nature. They don't define us. They aren't us.

Another thing I'd been crippled by for years was self-doubt. Self-doubt, I came to realise, is also an illusion of the ego. Once the ego fails to deceive you, you only begin to accept who you really are. Autism and Buddhism are very much the antithesis of one another in terms of their relation to the entity of the ego. Autism is, in essence, an extreme sense of egocentrism, whereas Buddhism seeks to vanquish the ego. It leads practitioners to an inner-freedom and a freedom to be able to stop thinking.

Autism is a heavy burden. It's a barrier to life, to being instinctive, free and spontaneous. It's at the extreme end of the human predicament of pretending to be an isolated individual, of pretending to be a separate self. People with autism have to go on a much more tortuous and far less accommodating road than most before they can discover their place, their own personal nirvana, and breathe a great sigh of relief.

Each week I turned up to the Catholic meditation group. I would work on applying the Buddhist psychology I was now inferring from several texts I'd become immersed in. Through hard-work, a daily regimen of meditation, and a strict adherence to the Noble Eightfold Path, I was becoming a better person—able to perform tasks with minimal effort yet maximal concentration, whilst maintaining a calm state of equanimity I'd never before have thought possible.

What I came to learn was that such practice wasn't going to cure me of my autistic traits, my anxieties or my depression. What gradual enlightenment was giving me was the strength to live nobly in the face of them, to never be overwhelmed by my own afflictions, to live deeply and fully and to ultimately realise that I am part of a much larger whole.

30. FROM AUTIST TO BUDDHIST

BUDDHIST PSYCHOLOGY awakens you to cosmic consciousness. The Middle Way facilitates a change of gears that enables you to slow down, allowing you to unlock who you really are. It creates a feeling of being awakened to the true state of affairs and unmasks the deception of our ego which creates an artificial, fragmented, diffused kind of awareness whereby you only pay attention to bits of things rather than the whole.

Egos are self-harming things but, once we learn to let it go, we can break free and become spontaneous. Spontaneity is liberation. It's also the opposite of being a rigid-thinking autist. Very often we autists tend to analyse things to death. Our brains seek patterns and we require very limited conceptual boxes to the fit the world into. Truth, however, is not found by picking the world to pieces. Accepting that life has no inherent meaning or purpose is the first step towards liberation.The bizarre fatalism of our monotheistic tradition that underpins our thinking in the West imbues us with fear, guilt and sadness. But Buddhism goes beyond this.

Just because I've read a few books on the subject, doesn't mean I identify as a Buddhist. For a start, I don't believe in karma or in reincarnation. I don't light incense to ward off evil spirits and I still eat fish and even a slice of prosciutto from time to time. Buddhist psychology, however, is something I have faith in. In essence, it is deeply practical, unconcerned with the supernatural, relentlessly logical and hard-edged. It's more akin to Western psychology than New Age spirituality. But unlike the Western methods, which view spontaneity and essential human nature with grave suspicion, Buddhism positively encourages spontaneity and the idea that our separateness is illusion—the idea we are separate egos contained in a separate body is said to detract from our essential nature. *We are all one consciousness experiencing itself subjectively*—to quote the magnificent Bill Hicks.

It's about being carefree and living in the moment. I don't fret about the future any more. I plan things yes, but I don't live in the cycle of endless craving and wanting like before. I don't worry if things don't go quite how I would've liked. I just accept it and keep going. My pleasure is in reclaiming the present moment. In waking up in the mornings and feeling the cold draught on my skin. In savouring the austere simplicity and wholesome flavour of a bowl of oats. In contemplating the interconnectedness of all phenomena, knowing that I'm part of a whole. Knowing that I am not 'I' at all, but am one with the birds, the trees and the pavement I tread during my mid-morning Sunday stroll to the Madeiran café to get a coffee and perhaps even a cinnamon-dusted custard tart.

Einstein, perhaps the most famous autist in history, had attained a sort of Bodhisattva-state through his intuitive grasp of natural phenomena. He could appreciate the sheer awe and wonder of what took place before his eyes. He'd reached a Zen level of understanding without, to anyone's knowledge, ever having come into contact with the practice or even showing the slightest propensity towards the Eastern religions. Buddhism doesn't have a monopoly on enlightenment, but it sure is one of the clearest guides to help you get there.

As long as I have food and shelter, I am content. I never worry or become snagged in the double-binds which propagate that inner-tension and anxiety which the Buddhists call *dukkha*. Embracing intuition, free from the endless torment of rigorous self-scrutiny, soothed all my afflictions and dissolved them. I am free to live life. Free of an illusory safety blanket. Free from the teddy bear of retreating into self. Free of becoming my own worst enemy by seeking security in things that would only prolong my own suffering. I am an autist but now I am also a Buddha. More to the point, I am an *Autistic Buddha* who took a long, winding, unorthodox road to the point where I could finally say: *Phew! Nothing in life is really that important.* Like Siddhartha Gautama himself who'd spent many self-defeating years as an overly-sensitive youngster seeking in vain to avoid affliction—a path that only hurt him and those around him (especially his loved ones)—I discovered the courage to be true to who I am, to become unified and to live vibrantly with everything around me.

If I were to pick a 'religion' though, it wouldn't be Buddhism. It would be the religion of compassion and kindness. Ultimately, love and kindness are what sustain human beings. Without them, human life is nothing. We need more of it in our world. When I meditate on love, to cultivate my softer side (the side that is most beneficial to others and the world around us), I think of my parents and how they kept going for the sake of both their sons. It was purely out of love they kept on supporting me and picking up the pieces after I'd messed things up. I also think of my ever-smiling grandmother and I picture the pure innocent visage of my brother, Jack, a dear soul blessed without fear and craving and always happy. If ever there was an angel in the flesh, it is him.

31. SIMPLE COMPASSION

I DON'T LIKE THE IDEA of a higher power. I don't believe in God, especially in the idea of a god watching over our every move, forever tallying our good and bad deeds and then punishing or rewarding us like a stern father figure once we float up to an imaginary afterlife in the sky. To me it's always been nonsense and I think such a belief creates silly religious one-upmanship that is unlikely to create mature self-actualised people.

I prefer to put my belief in simpler things like compassion. The sort of compassion not compelled by a need to please an imaginary deity, but one shared purely out of love without giving a thought to religious or social conventions. The story of Sujata, the simple milk maid who offered the then bony and starving ascetic Siddhartha Gautama a bowl of rice which the soon-to-be Buddha graciously accepted, makes much more sense than that of Jesus walking on water. Sujata eventually nursed Siddhartha back to good health by feeding and nourishing him. This simple act of compassion by a maid who demanded nothing in return, either from him or from the Gods she was supposed to worship at the time, touched the young Siddhartha. This simple act led him to take a different path from the ascetics around him practising a kind of mortification of the flesh. He realised that happiness in and of itself resided in simple acts of kindness. To me, such a simple philosophy for living made sense and I vowed to be kinder to those around me.

Altruistic behaviour is one of the best remedies to self-inflicted ills. It leads to a humbler, calmer self more able to connect with what is truly important. In my case, I had rarely been an altruist. My autistic traits had made me prone to self-absorption and it was about time I changed this, or at least tried to.

It started with my grandmother, whom I was back living with after my trip to China. I wasn't working at the time, so it seemed logical to buy her a hand-hoover. That was my first act of altruism. A hand-hoover that enabled her to vacuum up the dust on her stairs. I also cleaned her house from top-to-toe (it desperately needed it), made her bubble and squeak most nights and brought her back custard tarts from the Portuguese café every day.

It was a relief from being myself, concentrating solely on looking after my grandmother and not exacerbating my negatives. This altruistic component of our mental health, I came to realise, is something modern Western psychology fails to emphasise. Buddhism, on the other hand, recognises it as fundamental to optimal well-being.

Each day in town, I started to look outward a bit more.

I started to see people around me and imagined what difficulties they may be facing. There was a boy I saw every day in the library with cerebral palsy. He struggled up the steps, and even struggled to turn the pages of his favourite graphic novel which gave him pleasure in life. I contemplated his suffering and it made my own pale in comparison. To exacerbate what comparatively small problems I had by going into flight, locking myself indoors and shutting out the world, just seemed so insanely selfish now.

I also noticed a young Romanian girl who was selling the *Big Issue* outside the O2 shop. She was only young but would spend every other day braving the freezing cold just to make about ten pounds a day: to pay for her stay at the local hostel, a large can of Red Bull to keep her going, and one meal a day provided by the Salvation Army. Life was tough for her. Tougher than it had been for me. If I could have provided a simple solution to her suffering, I would have done. But at the time, I gave a pound each time I passed her, bought her a can of Red Bull and would chat to her for five minutes about how she was doing and what life was like back in Romania. It was the best I could do, and I sincerely hope it helped to brighten her day.

My grandmother's sister Colleen was in and out of hospital quite a bit during that time. She'd lived a lonely singular life and sought the company of others. I paid a visit to her flat each day, made her tea and brought round a raspberry doughnut from the local Polish deli down the road. This simple gesture brought her much happiness, I think.

The lady next to her, Pat, whose family it seemed never visited her in the ward, would talk to me and my aunt Colleen. Her dementia caused her to repeat stories quite often—such as the trip she did by steam locomotive from Toronto to Vancouver in her youth and her time spent volunteering to help the East End poor in a soup kitchen in Whitechapel—but she was undeniably charming and full of life despite the decrepit body she was inhabiting.

Her stay in hospital was to be a long one and, after my aunt had been discharged, it started to play on my mind that Pat was most likely lonely and not receiving any visitors. She was rotting away in hospital without anyone to show her love. So, I kept going to the hospital. Pat was of no relation to me, but it didn't matter. She just wanted to talk to somebody and, for an hour every other day, I let her chat away to her heart's content and tried to look interested despite hearing the same stories over and over again. I also brought her fudge and biscuits. I wasn't doing this to score brownie points with God, I was doing this because I wanted to. Because I was genuinely attuned to her pain. This, I learned, was a pure feeling of empathy, something previously alien to my experience.

32. THE BEAUTY OF IMPERFECTION

THE BEST THINGS in life aren't perfect and sym-metrical. More often than not we are attracted to the quirks and flaws in people and things. They are often the features we find most endearing and heart-warming. We may be moved by something as awe-inspiring and magnificent as the Sistine Chapel, but I doubt such a sight warms the heart in the same way as a crooked oak in the woods shedding its leaves in the fall.

We may speak highly of powerful successful people, and yet a simple kind gesture such as a friend cooking you a lumpy homemade casserole is infinitely more pro-found and has the ability to transcend every one of our insecurities.

We speak more fondly of a friend's peculiarities than his or her strengths. On our essential level, we are much like the nature around us: a fragile collection of cells at the mercy of the ravages of time and destruction. Once we acknowledge this fact, we can truly start living a lib-erated existence free from a persistent need to defy old age and the weaknesses in our characters or intellects. We can begin to live nobler, simpler lives based on pure love—the force that ultimately sustains all life. This is what Thoreau strived for by eliminating non-essentials and what Buddhist monks strive for when they renounce earthly possessions and desires.

For me, I was prepared to renounce that part of me that felt insecure and instead just live honestly. I decided that to be free was to stop running away and, the day that I did that, I arrived at my destination. While I may suffer because of my mental health problems, I can suffer in a dignified way. I can suffer with a smile on my face and a resounding faith that ultimately—despite any temporary hardships—love will prevail.

33. MY PAKISTANI FRIENDS

DURING MY TIME up in Nottingham, most of it spent in my room, I had actually done a fair amount of reading (very little of which was related to my degree). Despite an existence confined largely to four oppressive walls, there was a part of my depressed brain that still craved facts, knowledge and wisdom of the sort I knew I wouldn't be able to find in a search engine or on YouTube and had to actually go outside to find.

I'd sought some sort of answer to the meaning of life at one stage in the Bible, but fell asleep reading the New Testament. After a brief encounter with representatives from the Islamic Society, I started to read the Koran. I was struck by the simplicity and seductiveness of its message and also by its severity. I like Muslims. I like their modesty and I like their profound unyielding faith in God. Moreover, I like the Koran's egalitarianism and its power to inspire brotherhood.

When the Islamic Society had an event at the university, I went along to the Portland Atrium where it was held. Each Islamic country had a stall with friendly and enthusiastic representatives on hand to bombard you with facts about their homeland and offer morsels of delicious food such as date pastries from Oman, hummus from Palestine and *nasi goreng* from Indonesia. Foods from Central and South East Asia, the Middle East and Africa were in abundance there. Muslims are renowned the world over for their hospitality and generosity.

It was there I met Rehan, a skinny Pakistani engineering student with a wispy beard, and Basharat his roommate, also a Pakistani but much taller and darker. Rehan was from a well-off family in Karachi whereas Basharat, or Mr Hussein as he introduced himself, was from a poor rural background in Kashmir. Rehan was a devout Muslim who took his faith very seriously, whereas Basharat was a bit more flexible in his views. When I first introduced myself as an agnostic, I was sure they would want to convert me.

The reality was, upon discovering I was a foodie, they wanted to invite me to their house in Beeston for a slap-up feast of traditional Pakistani dishes. They did just that and I gleefully accepted their invitation. At the dinner, there was no talk of religion or the metaphysical. We just enjoyed one another's company. Basharat, a Zen master in the art of chappati making, did most of the cooking. It was a glorious meal consisting of fiery mutton and beef curries and pakoras with sides of rice and raita, followed by a cooling desert of *kheer*—a kind of rose-scented cardamom-infused rice pudding. I felt totally relaxed with these guys. We spoke fondly with each other about family, food and the cultural differences between the UK and Pakistan. When I told them about the drunken antics of British students, their eyes almost popped out of their heads. We all laughed about it. It was through a common passion for good food we enjoyed a wonderful evening. I regret not seeing them more often than I did when I was there. The quiet and modest company of those guys might have lifted me when I was at my lowest ebb. Their Islamic hospitality touched me, and my time spent with them had been all too brief. If we'd done that regularly, maybe it would've given me the strength to knuckle down. But I guess that's all in the past now. The best I can do is treasure the memory.

Recently I contacted them both in the hope of rekindling our friendship. I found out Rehan went back to Pakistan when the academic year was up. He's now working for a big engineering firm in his hometown of Karachi and is settling down. I wish him the best on his journey in life. Basharat is now living and working in Nottingham. I plan on visiting him soon, but this time I'll insist on cooking him a meal, perhaps an authentic British one. If he wants, we can eat it with chappatis. I know he enjoys making them a lot. To tell you the truth, I'm so excited to see him that when I do I'm going to give him a big hug.

34. AUTISM AND MY AFFINITY FOR FOREIGNERS

AS SOMEBODY with autism, I often feel like an outsider living on the fringes of mainstream society. My behaviours compared to that of the population majority are seen as so different, so alien to most people, that I'm quite often made to feel like a foreigner in my home country. A similar sense of outsiderism is also felt by many new arrivals to my native England, many of whom insulate themselves in their own ethnic and cultural bubbles to preserve their unique way of life and customs. It's for this reason that in my hometown of Bishop's Stortford, where roughly 25% of residents are foreign-born, I've tended to distance myself over the years from the town's British majority and have instead become closer to its vibrant minority communities with whom I share a similar sense of otherness.

Owing mainly to its proximity to London-Stansted Airport, the town is a veritable patchwork of multicultural groups living side by side: from Iranians to Italians and from Pakistanis to Poles. For someone like me who is so enthused by other cultures and the contributions they can bring to a host society, it's a fun place to be. One moment I'll be at the Sicilian cafe sipping espresso and nibbling cannoli next to elders from Corleone and Ragusa, then the next chowing down on homemade dhal and *khandvi* with East African Gujaratis who came to the UK to flee persecution.

The first person I got to know when I moved to Bishop's Stortford two years ago was Duarte, a Portuguese immigrant from the island of Madeira who originally came here to work as a truck driver. In the UK he met his wife, had a child and he now runs a successful bar and restaurant which specialises in the cuisine of his homeland. He's a very outgoing and amiable guy and we get on well—even with me being the awkward introvert I am. However, despite his material success here, he confides in me that he yearns for his island home, where the pace of life is slow, the people are warm and the food is superb. I also confide in him that Brits don't as a whole tolerate my eccentricities too well and often judge me negatively because of them. We both chuckle that Brits tend to be a pretty stuck-up and pompous bunch. To that we toast with a complimentary glass of passionfruit *poncha*, a delicious Madeiran liqueur made by Duarte himself.

In the company of him and his Portuguese expat pals, many of whom do menial jobs like factory work and

cleaning, I needn't be on my guard. They're totally relaxed about me, my eccentric nature, my autism and my
unconventional hand movements. It's simply not a big
deal to them which is cool.

The same is true of my friend Dawa, an Indian immigrant of Tibetan origin, who works as a postman in the
town and is well known among locals for his colourful
and eccentric persona. He arrived in the UK 15 years
ago and has striven to maintain his Buddhist placidity
and cheery Tibetan temperament in a culture known
for its cynicism and self-centredness. I first approached
Dawa when I bumped into him while shopping at a local Asian grocery shop. From his appearance, I couldn't
immediately guess where he originated, but after he told
me Tibet I immediately became enthusiastic and, like a
typical Aspie, unloaded a tonne of information on him
that I had absorbed recently from a stack of Buddhist
literature I'd been reading. Here was an authentic born-
and-bred Buddhist who was more than happy to chat to
me for hours on the subject, discussing everything from
samadhi to *sunyata*.

From then on, we've enjoyed tea and *tsampa*, a Tibetan staple of pounded barley, together at his home and
have waxed lyrical on Buddhist philosophy, the plight of
the Tibetan people, and even more banal topics like football, for hours on end. He confessed to me that most Brits
barely expressed any interest in his homeland, its unique

way of life and its rich Buddhist culture and tradition. In the 15 years he's been here, I was the first to enable him to share his world of compassion, meditation and prayer wheels which he spins religiously every morning to send out positive thoughts to those around him. Also, my autism isn't in the least bit problematic for him. If anything, he believes it has made me a more compassionate and richer person. In his company, my idiosyncrasies are less apparent and even seem mild in comparison.

For people with autism, finding our niche in a world that is often hostile to our very nature isn't easy. For many, this means finding common ground with fellow autistic and *neurodivergent* folk, but for me I tend to find common ground with those, who for different reasons, don't quite fit in as expected.

35. A LAST WORD

AS I FINISH the final pages of this book, I'm back in the same Hong Kong café I started in as a kid. At heart I'm still an incorrigible nostalgist, I guess. It's basic, utilitarian-chic here: formica tables and plastic seats like in one of the millions of roadside eateries in China. A tough-looking lady in a soy-spattered apron is making dumplings at the back. The clientele are all Chinese apart from me, the solitary geeky *gweilo*. To the left of my laptop is a glass of milky ying yang tea, to the right a plate of stir-fried tofu with green peppers. I periodically take bites using my chopsticks. My lips are covered in grease from the food and I'm gleefully happy. The people around me are from Fujian and Guangxi Provinces, I can tell from their South China accents. A few are old-school Hong-Kongers who are slowly being replaced by new arrivals from the Mainland. It's a delicious slice of British-Chinese life.

Sitting in this space, I realise I'm still basically the same person, but there's a key difference between the old and the new me: I'm free. I'm no longer attached to things. I can quite happily leave this place that I would have loathed to have left as a kid and still be happy. That is the key difference between then and now. Happiness doesn't mean having things. It means having achieved peace of mind, and being able to carry it with you wherever you go. It means contentment. It lies in accepting things the way they are and surrendering yourself to the fact you are nothing but a conscious bag of skin.

The only real important thing, clichéd as it may sound, is love. Knowing this, I won't be retreating into my room any longer. To be a Buddhist is to live nobly through affliction and to avoid causing unnecessary suffering to others—in my case my parents and others who love me—by avoiding the necessity to deal with it. The only thing that would inflict more suffering would be the psychological pain of going into flight again. I won't be putting my parents through hell again because I realise I love them too much. I will stand and fight and not run away, and I will do so with a smile on my face.

As I write this, I've decided to try to get in touch with my old pal Oliver. I found him on Facebook after all this time. I hope he's doing well—he certainly looks better in his profile picture than he did before. I also want to tell him how much better I'm doing now. Then I'm going to drop Wendy a line—she has a boyfriend now and is engaged to get married. I'm really happy for her. She deserves it. I want to congratulate her and wish her nothing but the best. And as for AJ? He's back in India and is keen for me to stay at his 'palace' and for his mum to cook me a vegetarian feast and her 'world-famous' *masala dhosa*. I look forward to that one day. I'm going to Skype call him in a bit from the café I'm in. After that, I'm going home on the Tube to Essex to meditate some more at home. Then maybe go for an espresso or, depending if they're in a festive mood or not, a glass of Madeiran passion fruit liqueur with my two new friends from church. This evening, I'll pay Pat, the old lady in hospital, a visit. She wants some Garibaldis, I think.

AFTERWORD

MEDITATION, like any skill, requires a lot of practice and perseverance. It's not what these self-help guides and relaxation tapes will have you believe. You don't switch off your brain by imagining yourself on a Bahamian island with white sandy beaches and warm turquoise waves lapping at your feet. It's firstly a process of stepping away mentally from the ceaseless bombardment of your thoughts, observing them from a distance and recognising their transient and elusive nature. Once you can sustain this feeling, you can fully concentrate on one thing.

My first object of concentration, which all Buddhist schools seem to emphasise for beginners, is the breath. Focusing on just breathing in and out proved a huge difficulty for me and at one stage I thought I would never be able to overcome it. As I started to breathe in and out, I would notice sounds outside like a car engine revving, a strimmer, birdsong, or my poor neglected stomach growling. Sounds have always disturbed me; even when sitting in the peaceful environs of a silent academic library the crunch of a page being turned over by somebody in the neighbouring study cubicle can seem un-bearable.

Eventually, after many frustrated attempts, I got bet-ter and better at just letting go and simply going with the in-and-out flow of air. The trick is to let yourself be-come distracted by things outside until the distractions die down and you can begin the real work of concentra-tion. Keeping the breath not too deep or too shallow but natural is also key. Eventually the maelstrom of mental chatter fades into the background and you feel yourself entering an empty space unencumbered by conditioned thought. You would think such an exercise would induce a gently lulling or somnolent effect, but in fact it actual-ly increases your alertness. Being less distracted by your inner-world, your perception of the outside phenomena becomes crystal clear.

Being an overly ambitious type, I at first attempted to meditate for 30 minutes at a time which was akin to mental torture. Sitting in the lotus proved not only pain-ful but also dangerous because I risked cutting off the cir-culation to my lower legs and feet. Subsequently I adopt-ed the semi-lotus which was also uncomfortable, though less likely to induce DVT, and then eventually I gave up sitting on the floor altogether and just sat in an unfash-ionably orthodox position in an upright chair. Gradually I shortened my 30-minute sessions to just 12 minutes which I found to be more than enough for a novice contemplative. Consistency, as with any form of practice like playing the piano or learning a new language, is the most important thing. Eventually 12 minutes became 20 which is now my minimum requirement for each day.

Unlike the Zen monks who rise at the un-Godly hour of 3am to recite sutras and meditate sometimes for 3 hours at a time barefoot in a cold room with tatami floors, I prefer to do mine after a period of activity, usually after I get home from work and have eaten dinner, and in the comfort of my warm carpeted bedroom. That way I can give it my undivided attention. If I were to do it in the mornings, there's always the chance I would nod off which wouldn't be a good thing, especially if I were to miss work.

Once you begin to grasp the technique of non-attachment to thoughts by focussing on the breath, you can gradually begin to meditate on the sort of positive emotions and feelings you wish to cultivate within you and sustain in your daily life. The Tibetan schools focus heavily on compassion, the motivating factor behind the Buddha's enlightenment, and encourages its practitioners to meditate on loving-kindness almost exclusively when going into retreat. The best way to do this is to first imagine a loved one and focus on them and allow feelings of unconditional love to fill your heart to the brim for 20 minutes or so. In my case, I meditate on each family member starting with my mum until I get to my beloved cat Smokey. While I would dispute dubious New Age claims that love can heal minds and bodies, it certainly increases a feeling of well-being. But in order to truly feel it and allow it to be the motivating force behind all your actions and interactions in daily life, it is vital you extend that love to the entire human family, even to those you dislike or regard as enemies. Recognising that we are all essentially the same despite being conditioned by different circumstances, cultures and religions, and that we are all appallingly fragile vulnerable creatures subject to the indisputable fact of impermanence, increases empathy and feelings of social connectedness.

These are two emotions that are often severely lacking, or even entirely absent, in people with autistic tendencies. So cultivating them through the simple practice of concentrating the mind proved invaluable in altering my hyper-cynical world view and my sense of isolation. It's through such practice you begin to realise you are not alone in your suffering. You begin to put yourself in others' shoes, imagine what they might be going through and what challenges and perhaps even heartache they face on a day-to-day basis. Such an attitude doesn't eradicate the pain you experience, but it does greatly reduce your negative response to such suffering and increases your resolve to relieve the suffering of others by being more altruistic, kinder and gentler.

As I maintained loving-kindness meditation for several weeks, my own suffering began to seem trivial in comparison to that of the world around me. I became more acutely aware of suffering in all forms experienced by others, from the young lady in my town with cerebral palsy to the painful boredom of those having to stack shelves at six in the morning at the local supermarket day in, day out often for years on end. You begin to feel their struggle, their pain, their exhaustion and this in turn reduces your response to your own suffering.

Such an attitude calms the inward tumult and transforms you over time into a person, much like His Holiness the Dalai Lama, who at the very core has others' interests at heart and who goes out of his way to achieve peace and harmony between people to reduce their suffering. Such a noble attitude can only be achieved by first filling your heart with kindness. Knowledge and intellect, while useful, are often useless without a caring and compassionate heart to go with it. As Aristotle said: *Educating the mind without educating the heart is no education at all.*

***

WHEN I first discovered Buddhism, I was looking for a way out of the squalid depths of despair the bitch-Goddess depression had thrown me into. Following the *dharmic* path enabled me to become more altruistic, compassionate and made falling into destructive patterns of self-absorption unlikely. However, I discovered a problem later on in my practice which began to trouble me and caused me to temporarily lapse back into a negative mind-set. Many Buddhists I began talking to struck me as so devout, so attached to Buddhism itself, as to appear wrapped up in their own self-image—wearing Buddhism almost as a fashion statement and idolising the dharma as an enlightened lifestyle above all others. This very egocentric attachment to Buddhism is problematic and a trap that many people seeking enlightened lifestyles, especially those from a Western background, fall into. Chogyam Trungpa, a famous Tibetan master, points these dangers out in his classic book *Cutting Through Spiritual Materialism* as does the Dalai Lama frequently in his speeches to foreign audiences whom he warns to guard against being attracted by the exotic patina of Eastern disciplines.

Another issue trap I fell into was to hoard Buddhist literature and to greedily devour books on the subject, to the point that the original Buddhist ethos of restraint and generosity was lost on me. I was consuming so much information on the subject that I began to lose the vital simple compassion that is so vital to Buddhist practice. I'd spend my evenings trying to get my head around impenetrable and arcane ideas in Zen and *Dzogchen* that I lost the time I could have spent feeding the birds, preparing my grandmother a nice supper, volunteering or doing charity work. My own depression actually returned slightly as soon as I began to agonise over the finer points of the dharma and how to reconcile certain concepts with my own secular Western world view.

Eventually, I gave up, let go and decided that reading too much into the subject of Buddhism is in and of itself problematic and vain. Now, instead of reading heavy-going and esoteric literature on the subject, or as soon as I begin to think too much about what can be a very esoteric discipline, I feed the birds, I make my grandmother tea, I tidy my room or I spend time preparing a simple meal—remaining mindful of what I am doing the entire time.

Whenever my mind strays, or I begin to feel anxious about reconciling elements of living an Eastern way of life in a Western environment, I focus on everything outside of me and realise how much I have to give to this world. The hungry birds need my kindness, my grandmother reciprocates the generosity I show her, and the earth says thank you when I recycle my cans.

In reality, I often see more altruism in those who grind through reality without ever pursuing a spiritual path than those who obsess over it. The local Afghan shopkeeper, for example, is in many ways a better Buddhist than those who meditate and chant mantras every day. The sweet-natured young man who works at the station helping disabled customers onto the train is in so many ways a far better Buddhist than me. In fact, *being Buddhist* means nothing if you aren't contributing to the well-being of others. It's merely a label with no inherent meaning if you wear it as fashion statement, you over-in-tellectualise it, or you boast about it to your friends.

The dharma must never be removed from complete-ly plain and ordinary everyday experience. That is vital. When someone the other day asked me what Buddhist rituals I do, I replied to them: *I make tea for my grand-mother*. In that simple action lies the essence of Bud-dhism.

Made in the USA
Middletown, DE
24 February 2024

50276919R00119